Dear Reader,

Let me invite you into a conversation between a mother and her daughter—*my* daughter, and my firstborn. Join us as we examine some of the real issues of life through the power of the fairy tale. Our hope is that you will discover what that master storyteller Hans Christian Andersen knew so long ago: "Every man's life is a fairy tale written by God's finger."

Use these letters to help you learn to fly again, to discover the magic in living out the greatest story ever written. Discover anew that we *can* slay the giants in our lives, and we have been given the power to break the "spell" that has bewitched mankind.

So, before the fairy dust settles, may these letters remind you that you really *are* a princess—the daughter of the most high King.

Janet Parshall

When the Fairy Dust Settles

A Mother and Her Daughter Discuss What Really Matters

Janet Parshall
and
Sarah Parshall Perry

NEW YORK BOSTON NASHVILLE

Unless otherwise indicated, all Scripture quotations are taken from
the HOLY BIBLE, NEW INTERNATIONAL VERSION®. NIV®.
Copyright © 1973, 1978, 1984 by International Bible Society. Used
by permission of Zondervan. All rights reserved.

Scriptures marked NASB are taken from the NEW AMERICAN
STANDARD BIBLE ®. Copyright © The Lockman Foundation
1960, 1962, 1963, 1968, 1971, 1972, 1973, 1975, 1977, 1995. Used by
permission.

Scriptures marked KJV are taken from the King James Version of
the Bible.

All names used in personal, anecdotal context in this book have
been changed to protect the anonymity of the parties represented.

Warner Faith
Time Warner Book Group
1271 Avenue of the Americas, New York, NY 10020
Visit our Web site at www.twbookmark.com

The Warner Faith name and logo are registered trademarks of
Warner Books.

Printed in the United States of America
First Warner Books printing: July 2004
10 9 8 7 6 5 4 3 2 1

Library of Congress Cataloging-in-Publication Data
Parshall, Janet.
    When the fairy dust settles : a mother and her daughter discuss
what really matters / Janet Parshall and Sarah Parshall Perry.
        p. cm.
    Includes bibliographical references.
    ISBN 0-446-69317-0
    1. Christian women—Religious life. I. Perry, Sarah Parshall.
II. Title.
    BV4527.P36 2004
    248.8'43—dc22   2004004973

Cover photo by David Hills.

We dedicate this book to our mothers and grandmothers, who have exemplified the attributes of perseverance, courage, and patience. In them we have seen the character of women who know what it means to love selflessly and unconditionally. To Margaret DiFrancesca and Barbara Combs, thank you for the immeasurable influence you have had on our hearts. You have created in us a hunger to be women of the Word, whose desire is to share it with the world.

We also dedicate this book to all women who have come to realize, and to those who have *yet* to discover, that following Jesus and living for Him is the most glorious of tales. It is the *one* story that does indeed allow us to live "happily ever after."

We must finally dedicate this work to Craig Parshall, husband, father, and novelist extraordinaire. We thank you for your hours of work as our *de facto* editor and primary literary mentor. You have planted in both of us a love of the written word, as well as a desire to use its power to expand the kingdom of the one true Prince.

Contents

※

Part 3 Relationships

Sugar and Spice, Not Everything's Nice

Part 4 Sex

Beware the Sirens, and Pipers with Rats

Part 5 Treasures

The Queen Was in the Counting House, Counting Out Her Money

Introduction

Once Upon Our Time

"Once upon a time..."

What magic is in those words! When we were young, stories that started out with this phrase filled us with images of kings and queens; they made us dream of fairies and dragons; we quaked at the tales of ugly witches and one-eyed giants. These words created in us an anticipation of the arrival of a handsome prince who would wake the sleeping princess and take her to live with him in the glorious castle on the hill. Without knowing all the details, we just *knew* they would live in splendor and immeasurable joy the rest of their lives. *Who knows, we thought, maybe that princess is me. Perhaps a handsome prince will show up at my front door and I will ride off with him in his golden carriage—and I just might live happily ever after.*

Then we grew up. Real life surrounded us like the brambles around Sleeping Beauty's castle. Things didn't happen the way they did in our storybooks. Maybe, traveling life's highway, we saw a lot of toads who told us they were really princes, but there was no way we would ever kiss them, no matter how much they promised to change.

We came to realize that in real life, sometimes there really are wicked stepmothers and -fathers, and bosses, and friends, and coworkers. We waited for Tinkerbell to sprinkle us with fairy dust so we could fly away. But instead we found ourselves locked in bad rush-hour traffic.

Fairy tales are the stuff of dreams, the promise that the best is yet to be. They plant in our hearts the longing for a great adventure and the desire to travel to faraway places.

Everything seems to work out all right in a fairy tale. Good is always rewarded, and evil is constantly defeated. The little peasant is often, in the end, more powerful than the king. And nasty witches melt away.

But somehow, somewhere along the way, we lost the magic. The heavy boots of reality frequently trampled on our dreams. As grown women, we came to realize that we would never be princesses who lived on royal estates, somewhere on picturesque hills; we might have to settle for apartments. We would probably never own a goose that would lay a golden egg, and we couldn't spin straw into gold, so we had to get jobs. We didn't have three wishes granted to us, so we piled up debt on our credit cards and wished the balances weren't so high.

But most painfully, we started to question whether anyone *really* lives "happily ever after." What is the real power of the fairy tale? Why have these stories endured over hundreds of years? Why do we, as women, still feel pulled back to the magic and the message of these fables?

G. K. Chesterton described the power this way: "Fairy tales are more than true: not because they tell us that dragons exist, but because they tell us that dragons can be beaten."

Fairy tales are, in truth, morality tales. They teach us something about life and how to respond to the challenges we all experience along the way to the proverbial happy ending. Greed, fear, lust, courage, strength, passion, and love are the elements not only of these stories but also of the human experience. How do we live rightly, then, and not fall prey to the giants and trolls of life? Is there some power available to us that doesn't come from fairies and elves, but from a more magnificent and enduring source? Is it possible for someone to become "royalty" in a sense, even if she is not born into it?

Being in radio has given me (Janet) the opportunity to hear what is going on in the human heart. I listen to adults who miss the magic and have forgotten the myth. They no longer remember what it is like to feel the lightness of childhood. When Captain Hook asked Peter Pan, in J. M. Barrie's classic *Peter Pan*, "Who and what art thou?" Peter responded, "I'm youth, I'm joy. I'm a little bird that has broken out of the egg." Far too many of us have *not* broken out of the egg—we're just scrambled!

I loved reading fairy tales to my children. They sat on the edge of the bed with wide eyes and slack mouths, mesmerized by the stories of flying carpets and animal musicians. I watched their eyes sparkle, knowing these myths were planting in their hearts the seeds of the greatest story of all—the one each of us has the opportunity not only to read but to *live*. It's a story that has kings and princes, magnificent beasts of the ocean, and giants who are felled by a shepherd boy. It's a story where an evil sorcerer works his magic until confronted by the miracles of a carpenter King. It is the Great Tale: where donkeys talk, oceans divide, and finally, death is conquered.

What happens when real life crashes into the dreams of childhood? Can the fairy tales of childhood rekindle in us a sense of adventure? Are they still able to spur us on to a noble cause? Can they create in us the courage to begin a journey when its path lies through a dark and scary wood?

Let me invite you into a conversation between a mother and her daughter—*my* daughter, and my firstborn. Join us as we examine some of the real issues of life through the power of the fairy tale. Our hope is that you will discover what that master storyteller Hans Christian Andersen knew so long ago: "Every man's life is a fairy tale written by God's finger."

Use these letters to help you learn to fly again, to discover the magic in living out the greatest story ever written. Discover anew that we *can* slay the giants in our lives, and we

have been given the power to break the "spell" that has bewitched mankind.

So, before the fairy dust settles, may these letters remind
you that you really *are* a princess, the daughter of the most
high King.

Part 1

Beauty

The Body-Image Beast

"Fairyland is nothing but the sunny country of
common sense."

—G. K. CHESTERTON

-ò-

Beauty and the Modern Woman

Darling daughter:

Have I ever told you how beautiful you are? No, don't roll your eyes like that. I mean it. This is not just your mother talking. You really are breathtaking. In fact, let me share a little secret with you.

One of the things I love to do when you and I walk into a room together is to enter just behind you. This way you can't see that I am watching the reactions of other people as they look at you. Tall, thin, blonde, blue-eyed, dimpled . . . sounds like a description out of some women's magazine. But there you are, in all your beauty.

I will never forget the day you were born. Daddy and I looked at each other just after you made your arrival and said, "Where did she get *those* looks? Are you sure we have the right baby?"

There is no question you have been blessed in the area of

looks. And I do mean *blessed*. Some people have them, and some don't. So let me ask you a question—heart to heart. Do *you* think that God does, in fact, bless some people with looks? Or is it all happenstance and genetic pooling? If God knows when every sparrow falls and can count the number of hairs on your head (and yes, you *did* get my thin hair, so I guess He has fewer hairs to count for both of us!), then does He purposely give some people good looks?

Think of all the people in Scripture who are defined by their looks: Rachel ("lovely in form, and beautiful"), Joseph ("well-built and handsome"), Bathsheba ("the woman was very beautiful"), Rebekah ("very beautiful"), Esther ("lovely in form and features"), and, of course, Sarah (her own husband said "what a beautiful woman you are"), just to name a few. Yet the most important person in Scripture, described in that verbal oil portrait found in Isaiah, "had no beauty or majesty to attract us to him, / nothing in his appearance that we should desire him" (53:2).

Makes me wonder: how important are looks? Does God give them to certain people because that gift will be part of a bigger plan the Creator has designed just for them? Does He bestow beauty on some because they will have a public ministry and an attractive face will be a necessary tool? Or does He give His beautiful creation this gift so that the gifted can learn humility?

But on occasion beauty can cause trouble, as some fairy

tales tell us. I loved story time when you were little. And I loved the way you adored fairy tales. You and your sister loved to play princess, complete with blankets for capes and cardboard for crowns. The classics were your favorites, and "Snow White" was near the top of the list.

When you think about it, this tale is more about pride and envy than it is about seven little people. Here was this beauty who was described as having skin as white as snow, lips as red as blood, and hair as black as ebony—a real medieval knock-out.

But she had this problem with her stepmother (it *always* goes back to the mother). The stepmom was also beautiful and couldn't stand anyone challenging her in the area of looks, so she had this running dialogue with her mirror that could not tell a lie. She'd say, "Mirror, mirror on the wall, who is the fairest of them all?"

And the mirror would reply, "Fair Queen, you are the fairest of them all."

As long as the stepmother got the answer she wanted— "It's *you*, baby, it's all about you!" (that would be the modern translation)—then things were good in her world. Her beauty was what defined her and got her out of bed in the morning.

But life is never that simple, even in fairy tales. Things change, especially looks. You know what happened. One day the queen started her daily ritual of mirror talking, and she got lip from the mirror: "Queen, you are very fair, 'tis true, but Snow White is a thousand times fairer than you."

Uh-oh. Things were going to get rough. Did he have to rub it in? Couldn't the old looking glass just have said "more fair" or "a little fairer"? But that "thousand times" stuff. Really!

You recall things went downhill from there. Fold in dwarfs, poison apples, a long sleep, a glass coffin, and, of course, a gorgeous prince (did you really expect this man to be homely?), and what happened? The story ends with the stepmom being so full of hate and jealousy that her heart burst—leaving Snow White and her prince to—here it comes—"live happily ever after."

Beauty. In this story it was both a blessing and a curse. So now, my beauty, I want to hear your heart. Why do some people have it and some don't? Does God ordain how we will look? Does He care if, unlike the rest of us, He looks also on the "inward appearance"?

I can't wait to see how you reply. In the meantime, here is a little motherly advice: don't take any apples from strangers.

Love you!

Mom:

Once, when I was about twelve or so, I asked you, "What

will I look like when I grow up?" You answered sweetly but honestly, "Like you do now, only bigger." I was so disappointed! In my mind, I was waiting for the transformation.

Like Cinderella, the scullery maid who became a princess, I honestly believed there was a point in my life where I would wake up and find I had suddenly become the embodiment of Walt Disney beauty. From the ugly duckling to Beauty and the Beast to the frog prince, folklore is full of tales of the awkward and the ugly becoming elegant and striking. I was hoping the same thing would happen to the gawky preteen with the dirty-blonde hair. It never dawned on me that God might not have that kind of beauty in mind for me.

I blame it on fairy tales. Curse those cardboard crowns!

Even spectacular women struggle with their looks. Ah! But how much less they struggle! Take Gisele Bündchen (a supermodel—and I feel compelled to tell you that *only* because you don't follow models like baseball players . . . the way I do), for example. I can't imagine she gets up in the morning and bemoans her forty-eight-inch legs and flowing chestnut hair. But *why* is she beautiful? I've seen her parents. They're nice, average-looking people—but not necessarily possessed of superior genetics themselves.

So, I figure it has to be God.

If it's true that "[God] created my inmost being; [He] knit me together in my mother's womb" (Ps. 139:13), then He had to know what I was going to look like, and He had to have planned it that way.

I don't think anyone would debate that beauty is a gift. As it says in James, "Every good and perfect gift is from above" (1:17). Beauty seems pretty good *and* rather perfect, don't you think? In fact, beauty is itself a very *unique* gift. Unlike talent, intellect, wealth, or status—which can, to some degree, be tweaked by our own efforts—beauty is a kind of reward "obvious" to everyone, making God the only logical source.

Beauty is the "out there" gift. Sure, you can work at smoothing out the rough edges, but when it comes right down to it, you either have it or you don't.

So why would God give that kind of gift to some people and not to others? Especially when He knows it might cause pain and bitterness? Take Rachel and Leah, for example. "Leah had weak eyes, but Rachel was lovely in form, and beautiful" (Gen. 29:17). To make matters worse, Laban, the girls' dad, decided he was going to pull the old switcheroo with the ugly one on Jacob's wedding night—after Jacob had slaved for seven years to get the beautiful one. I bet *that* was the catfight heard round the world.

When a gift like beauty is so obvious, so desired, so hotly contested, and so rare, God has to have a plan in mind when He gives it to one and not the other. (Otherwise, He would simply be unfair!) Even with the Bible's greatest lookers, their beauty wasn't just a happy coincidence. There was always a goal of God's behind it. Look at Esther. By making her the fairest in the land, God allowed King Xerxes to fall in love with her, dethrone Queen Vashti, and ultimately save the Jews from Haman's vicious plot.

I thought about this verse today: "Each one should use whatever gift he has received to serve others, faithfully administering God's grace in its various forms" (1 Pet. 4:10). It seems to me that God's gifts don't really belong to us. They're on loan, actually. And they're all supposed to be put to use for the kingdom. The woman with riches contributes. The woman with leadership leads. The woman with mercy comforts.

And the beautiful woman?

Well, I think she does what the Lord leads her to do: speaking, singing, ministering, carpooling, or just doing the dishes. Because who knows? The Lord may just use that beauty to attract the lost or save a nation.

But here's my question: what happens when the beauty fades?

"Charm is deceptive, and beauty is fleeting; / but a woman who fears the LORD is to be praised" (Prov. 31:30). While the Lord blesses some with beauty, He reinforces that it can never last—so, in a way, that beauty is both a blessing and a curse.

If God's plan is to give you the "curse" of beauty (oh, that we were all so fortunate!), what happens when the gift becomes more important than the Giver? How do you prevent the way you look from becoming the most important part of how you see yourself, especially when it's often the most obvious quality about you?

Love,

your five-foot, seven-inch-tall daughter with the strawberry birthmark, blue eyes, and straight, blonde hair

My beauty (for you are):

Thank you for thinking so deeply on the subject of our outward appearance. I think you are really asking two important questions. The first is whether or not beauty is as divinely predetermined as, say, what sex we will be. Second, since man does look so intently on the outside, and not on the heart, as our Father does, are we able to prevent our looks from becoming the ultimate self-definer in such an image-conscious world?

If you and I believe in the sovereignty of God in *all* things, then we must necessarily believe our physical appearance is equally predetermined. Whether or not we have blue eyes or black hair is either simply biology, or it is as much a part of the "knitting" together of who we are in our mothers' wombs as any other part of us is.

I choose to believe He is Lord of all. It follows that my eyes, my nose, and my hair color (in my case, the color I was born with, as opposed to the one that comes in a box) were all decided way before I was even conceived. Don't you love that thought? God loves us so much that He, and He alone, chose our original colors!

A while back, all of my friends were having their "colors" done. A person's color was categorized as one of the seasons: I'm a "summer," I'm a "fall," and so on. Your color determined what sort of a wardrobe you should wear by predetermining what colors looked best on you. (For the record, my color is confused, because I just buy what's on sale!)

But in truth, your colors have already been done. The Master, with one stroke of His brush, painted you just the way He wanted you. Some He paints as gorgeous portraits, others He designs as plainer pieces, but all of His creatures carry the touch of the Artist's perfection. Why? Because we are designed in His image. When you think about it, that makes us all truly beautiful.

David said in one of his psalms that he wanted to "gaze upon the beauty of the LORD" (27:4). Since God is spirit and not in a physical form, what was David looking at? This goes to your second question. Where do we really find beauty: on the face or in the heart?

One of the master tellers of fairy tales was Hans Christian

Andersen. He understood the power of myth to underscore a truth in life.

He told the story of a little critter who struggled with his appearance. The other birds living around the pond shunned this ugly duckling. Andersen wrote:

> Everyone was mean to the ugly duckling. Some ducks bit him. Some made fun of him. The chickens and geese teased him and bullied him. And the turkey cock, who acted as if he were king of the barnyard, said, "That duckling is so ugly I can't bear to look at him." Then he flew at the duckling and scratched him with his claws.[1]

His siblings started to treat him unkindly, and so did an old tomcat and a prize hen. Sadly, this little one saw himself as others saw him—ugly. In fact, Andersen said the little duckling grew ashamed of his appearance. Like so many of us, this creature allowed others to define him as *they* saw him, not as he truly was.

As happens in fairy tales (and in real life), time passed, and things changed. Winter slowly turned into spring, and the little duckling's real nature was revealed. He became a majestic swan—the most beautiful of all the barnyard creatures! Beneath what some thought was ugliness lay magnificent beauty.

Think of all the people who walk around in our lives that at first blush seem to be ugly ducklings. But their real characters are clothed in breathless beauty. Oh, that God would give us His eyes to see others (and ourselves) that way. We have all heard this story time and time again, but in these days of hyper body awareness, we have forgotten true beauty resides within and not without. My mother told me that, and now I'm telling you—again.

David wanted to spend time gazing at God because of God's heart. God's Spirit, by the way, is the only one of which it is said, "God is love." The psalmist wanted to focus on God's love because he saw himself being loved in return. That is the definition of beauty: not cosmetics, or fashion, or surgical alterations, but the condition of your heart.

Her face bore the marks of hard work, long hours, and brutal conditions. But the "untouchables" of Calcutta saw only true beauty when Mother Teresa held them in her arms. Her heart outdistanced her appearance.

His skin was like leather after years of working over the side of a boat in rough seas and salty air. But the One in whose heart he found favor loved Peter, the fisherman. This disciple was able to see the beauty of Christ in him because he learned the lessons of forgiveness and unconditional love.

Sometimes these life lessons are taught so often that we grow dull of hearing. But right now, while I can, let me tell you one more time: you are *so* beautiful. Yes, the Master has painted you with breathtaking colors—blonde hair, blue eyes, rosy dimples. It's all perfectly put together because the God of perfection chose to design you that way.

But your true beauty is your heart—your desire to be like Him. Your gentle, loving, and forgiving spirit allows me to see Jesus in you. Even when your external beauty fades—and it will—you will still be beautiful. When your blue eyes grow dim and your blonde hair has turned gray, you will still be spectacular because you gaze upon the Lord, and His beauty is reflecting back on you.

I thank God for His beauty in you.

Mama

2

Dress and Fashion

Dearest daughter:

As I write this to you, I am sitting in a café in Washington, D.C. It is morning. Rush-hour traffic has started to die down, and folks are coming up from the metro to walk to their jobs. It's summer—and it's hot and muggy. Remember, the nation's capital was built on a swamp.

Darling daughter, as I watch the people go by, particularly the women, I have to remind myself I am in a major metropolitan city and not at the beach. Hemlines up, necklines down, backs of blouses missing, see-through material. Men rush past, then turn around quickly for a second look. Is it just a look or the beginning of lust? Is the woman culpable here? Is she making a fashion statement or sending a signal?

I know my generation is older than yours, but some concepts transcend time. Maybe this one does. So I'd love your thoughts. You are, after all, a real princess, the daughter of the King of all kings.

As I've often told you, your name, Sarah, means

"princess." From the moment of your conception, we knew you would be our princess (or prince—no routine ultrasound pictures for Mom and Dad back then). But we purposely gave you the name of Abraham's wife.

She was beautiful, just like you; in fact, she was so stunning that Abram (he hadn't received his name change yet) took her to Egypt, and Pharaoh went gaga over her. Abram got sheep, cattle, donkeys, camels, and even servants because of Sarai (she hadn't yet received her divinely transformed name yet either). To quote you, Sarai "rocked."

I can hear you now: "Enough already with the Bible lesson—what's the point?"

Here's the point: how do you think Sarah adorned herself? You know, dressed herself, did her hair, pierced her ears (or nose)? Did she wear makeup? The best Elizabeth Arden (or would that be *Elisabet Ardenai?*) of the day?

I don't believe in majoring in the minors, but how do you think a woman after God's own heart should adorn herself? What do our clothing choices say about who we are on the inside? In a sensate, postmodern, sex-saturated, sin-sick culture, are there right and wrong choices about dress and clothing styles?

Tell me your thoughts on adorning the modern female. Do you have a standard for your clothing decisions? Is there much discussion among your peers on this, or am I just an old fuddy-duddy whose age is showing?

Tell me, because I care what you have to say.

Because I love you.

Mom

Mama:

I got your letter yesterday and laughed when you said it was hot and muggy. I know it all too well—I'm only a few hours north of you in Maryland, after all. I spend mornings like this one wondering what to wear so I can make it from my car to my office without breaking a sweat. So I thought about your question as I stared at my open closet this morning.

How does a woman after God's own heart adorn herself? Well, I suppose my perspective is a little more liberal than yours. While I am a bit of a fashionista (there's a new word for your generation!), I also have a tendency to view clothing options as a part of our total and *complete freedom* in Christ. I don't like to be restricted, and I don't see anything wrong with dressing to make a statement—it just depends *what* that statement is.

Remember the dress code at my Christian college? Do you also remember how, more than once, I was issued demerits by my R.A. (resident assistant) for a too-short skirt length or for wearing slacks to class? At the time, I was angry at the university for not letting me express myself and for removing a part of my personal freedom.

It seems to me that a dress code is a completely different matter for a woman than it is for a man. The fundamental pieces of a man's costume are always the same. Not so for a woman. There are endless clothing combinations that require varying degrees of modesty. Today, thankfully, I've got the freedom to wear whatever I want. But that also means how I dress now is regulated only by what the Lord thinks— not what a school or employer requires. It also means what I wear is reflective of how I see myself: am I professional? a sophisticate? relaxed? modest? a trendsetter?

I thought about this verse when reading your letter: "Your beauty should not come from outward adornment, such as braided hair and the wearing of gold jewelry and fine clothes. Instead, it should be that of your inner self, the unfading beauty of a gentle and quiet spirit, which is of great worth in God's sight" (1 Pet. 3:3–4).

I *know* the key to real beauty doesn't stem from my physical appearance, but there are mornings where a particularly clever outfit gives me an edge; I feel stronger and more confident because I feel I look good (fairly wrong thinking, if you ask me). I've thought about why God took it upon Himself to remind women, and *only* women, exactly what beauty is *not*. He must have known women would struggle so much with their appearances. Unlike men, we're not content to take a passing glance in the mirror before leaving for work, just to make sure we have nothing stuck in our teeth! (I wish I had my husband's nonchalance when it comes to dressing. Only this morning, he held up a blue shirt and khaki slacks and asked, "Does this match?" This is as far as his formula for dressing goes.) Maybe God understood that a woman's appearance, unlike that of a man, would go frequently to the fundamental issue of who she is.

But does God fault us for wanting to look good? Does He condemn me for the desire to please my husband or positively represent my employer or shine on my wedding day? Does He frown when I want to make a statement about my personal style with a particularly bold clothing combination? I can't believe God meant such things to have no importance to us, but where does a woman draw the line?

You are careful about your appearance and *always* manage to look put-together and stylish. But you also don't make a Kate Spade handbag or a perfect hairdo your highest priority. Where is the balance for you?

Much love,

Sarah

P.S. This morning, I settled on a sage-green blouse and a gray, knee-length skirt. I think my R.A. would be proud.

Hello, darling:

I was pleased to see you feel that dressing *does* make a statement. And I was also pleased to see the question really is: *what* statement?

In Washington, there is an unstated dress code. For example, women who work on Capitol Hill always dress in professional outfits (dresses and pantsuits). Lobbying groups, special-interest representatives, and reporters all have a certain air of fashion because they all *do* want to make a statement.

But so do Britney Spears and Madonna (thank you, thank you, and thank you for *not* wanting to make *their* statement!).

Actually (and here is the challenging part of the mother/daughter relationship), I question your statement that "what I wear is reflective of how I see myself." Shouldn't it be reversed, so that what we wear is really how we want others to see us—or more to the point, see Jesus *in* us?

We serve a God of grace and mercy who loves us unconditionally, and He made us women by divine design, not by accident. I do think the One who blew the stars into existence does care about this adornment issue.

Yes, we have liberty in Jesus. Galatians speaks exactly to this issue, where Paul said that it is "for freedom that Christ has set us free" (5:1). But 1 Peter also talks about a kind of adornment: "Live as free men, but do not use your freedom as a *cover-up* for evil; live as servants of God" (2:16, emphasis mine).

He was talking about the adornment of a cover-up. In other words, my precious daughter, I think the principal to be gleaned here is that we have the liberty to dress like street-walkers if we want, but is that what we want people to see in us? Will my adornment choices get in the way of people seeing Jesus in me?

You rightly asked about the question of balance (I have such a smart daughter!), and I think that is really the key. When I make decisions about my dress, I ask myself some questions:

- Whom am I dressing for: Him or me?
- Will I be (in this order) modest, comfortable, fashionable? (Notice the comfort issue appears before fashion. Does that say something about my age or what?)
- What's appropriate for the situation? No swimsuits or shorts in church services or on Capitol Hill, and I don't think a plunging neckline is a good idea on CNN.
- How will my adornment decisions affect the people I am around? For example, if I am speaking at a church that has an issue with women wearing pantsuits (no matter who the designer might be, or how expensive), if it is an issue

for that group, I won't wear a pantsuit. I might be more comfortable, it might travel better in a suitcase, and I might like it more. But if I want first to serve Him and His people, then I let it go. I have the liberty to wear what I want, but I have the love for Him and His people that sets my liberty aside for the sake of the gospel.

When you think about it, sweet lamb, our adornment issues might really be more about how we adorn our hearts than how we adorn our bodies. If we say out loud, boldly, with a heart on fire, "In him we live and move and have our being" (Acts 17:28), then our fashion decisions become more a reflection of our hearts in Him rather than of the latest designs from Milan, Paris, and London. (Don't get me wrong. I would love to have the time and the checkbook to get some of those threads. But I don't want the catwalk to be the way to my heart—I want my heart to be the pathway to His beauty and grace.)

I think God cares about our decisions of adornment. He is our Father, and just as your earthly daddy always cared about how you looked when you went out the door (because dressing *does* make a statement, and boys *do* look), God cares about what statement we are making as well.

As a woman, what statement are you making? What statement are you *trying* to make? What are you saying with your dress? This is not a rhetorical question—I really want to know, if for no other reason than I, too, might want to add *fashionista* to my name.

Love,

Mom

Mom:

I have a tank top I bought in Greenwich Village on a trip to New York. I don't know if you've ever seen it, but it bears the image of a grinning skeleton with the word "Bony" printed underneath. I like it partly because of its irony (after all, it's a *skeleton* that's being described as bony), and partly because it's different. It's atypical. It's out of the ordinary. It makes a statement. I came across this shirt in the laundry after reading your letter, and I realized what this whole issue of dress comes down to for me: on the one hand, it really doesn't matter what I wear, and yet, on the other, it matters a great deal what I wear.

Let me explain.

We've both agreed that rule number one in the dress of the modern Christian woman is to reflect the Lord and not dishonor Him. But God loves us despite our outfits, our hairstyles, our makeup, and our jewelry. Our dress matters nothing to Him as far as His love for us is concerned.

Then I got to thinking about Adam and Eve in the garden, after the Fall: "Then the eyes of both of them were opened, and they realized they were naked; so they sewed fig leaves together and made coverings for themselves" (Gen. 3:7). Adam and Eve were able to determine for themselves that a covering was needed, because they were ashamed: "[Adam] answered, 'I heard you in the garden, and I was afraid because I was naked; so I hid'" (Gen. 3:10). In fact, it was only after He saw His kids fumbling around with fig leaves that God showed them animal skins would work better as a covering (Gen. 3:21). (Now, I know there is a deep theological reason as to why He chose animal skins. But I can almost hear Him chiding Adam and Eve, "Well, if you're going to put something on, at least wear something that fits!")

I also had another thought. We studied 1 Corinthians 11:2–16 in church Sunday morning. In that passage, Paul discussed the necessity of women's covering their heads during worship, which seems restricting (I'm thinking of my dress code in college again). But if you study history, you learn that some of the women in the church at Corinth may have originally come from pagan backgrounds, where their hair was wild during "worship," and they had brought these practices with them into their new Christian faith.

Paul began this chapter by discussing the distinction between men and women and how "the head of every man is Christ, and the head of the woman is man, and the head of

Christ is God," so that "the woman ought to have a sign of authority on her head" (1 Cor. 11: 3, 10). In other words, *dress* was used as a symbol that women were under the leadership of their husbands.

But Paul also made another, less-obvious point in this passage—he was encouraging the body of Christ to keep the emphasis on the main thing: *God.* Paul didn't want the Corinthians to be distracted by, among other things, one another's dress while their attention was supposed to be focused on the Lord. So he instructed them:

> *Judge for yourselves: Is it proper for a woman to pray to God with her head uncovered? Does not the very nature of things teach you that if a man has long hair, it is a disgrace to him, but that if a woman has long hair, it is her glory? For long hair is given to her as a covering. If anyone wants to be contentious about this, we have no other practice—nor do the churches of God.* —(I COR. II:13–16)

I hear Paul saying here, "Don't make each other stumble. Focus on God. Then, aside from that, wear what you want."

So, short of dishonoring God with our dress, could it be that Christians make more out of restrictions on dress than they should? Does the difference of one inch on a hemline have *that much* of an impact on a man passing by? Does a pantsuit on a woman *really* obscure her femininity? Does it *truly* matter if a woman wears a modest two-piece bathing suit on a family boating trip?

I don't think it does!

But on the other hand, it seems to me that God gave us the freedom to *make it matter, if we want it to!* I wrote you in my first letter about the kind of freedom I have when I decide what to wear. But this kind of freedom goes beyond not having to adhere to a dress code. God is a creative, infinite, and colorful God. He's the God of wool, silk, cashmere, and rayon—just as He's the God of chartreuse, violet, maize, and peach. Every fabric, color, and texture in the universe comes from the same God who decided that one species of bird wasn't interesting enough and so made five hundred of them!

I am happy the Lord knew us as His children so well that He understood how quickly we would get bored with wearing the same things over and over. The God who recognizes that trends come and go is the same God who made me a visual creature with a penchant for pretty outfits (and shopping . . . but that's another letter). So He threw the whole world of clothing open to me and said, "Take your pick."

Now, I can't guarantee that I have *taste*, and that I will make sophisticated choices with all this freedom, but I suppose I have the freedom to be ridiculous and garish too.

So, as to your question: What statement am I making with my dress?

Statement #1: I am a Christian.

Statement #2: It really doesn't matter that much what I wear. I will always be a Christian, and God will always love me.

Statement #3: I am creative, colorful, and unique. God made me this way. Even more important, *God is that way*! And the God who made me approves of my expressing all this every day when I pick out something to wear.

Now, you'll have to excuse me. It's getting close to my bedtime, and I still have to iron the pink peasant blouse that I'll wear tomorrow with my red plaid pants . . . and my army boots.

Love,

Sarah

3

Plastic Surgery and Body Makeovers

Dear Mom:

I am having one of those days. You know, when you feel as if you've gained ten pounds overnight, and all the clothing you own is waging a silent war against you when you squeeze into it. I caught sight of my meandering thighs in the mirror this morning and stepped squarely on the cat, I was so appalled.

And don't get me started on my hair. Grandpa Parshall's bald head had better body.

I'm not a millionaire, an heiress, or an actress. I don't have thousands of dollars at my disposal, and I don't consider myself particularly vain. But I've actually thought, at different times and for different reasons, about plastic surgery. A tummy tuck, rhinoplasty, you name it. And because you don't have to be rich and famous anymore to get plastic surgery, the possibility seems not only a little more accessible, but a little more appealing too. In fact, any woman on the Web can find a cosmetic surgeon for what ails her. Jane Does all over the country are foregoing their yearly vacations and minivan upgrades for a bigger chest or a flatter gut.

And watching TV doesn't help, either. Oh no—I'm not just talking about the legions of lovelies that parade across "must-see TV." I'm talking about shows dedicated to normal, everyday people getting plastic surgery. ABC's *Extreme Makeover* promises not just a haircut, makeup application, and wardrobe change, but various and numerous plastic-surgery procedures as well. In addition to off-the-charts ratings, the producers have received over ten thousand applications from people eager to be patients on the show![1] That's ten-thousand-plus people willing to go under the knife for beauty.

So it seems that everybody's doing it. The culture embraces it. And the Bible doesn't specifically condemn it—after all, it wasn't a consideration in the early Christian church.

Assuming I have the money, what's stopping me?

I've heard some Christians complain that spending thousands of dollars on plastic surgery is just plain foolish when the church needs so much support, and the money could be used to further God's kingdom. Wrong. After all, if that's the case, I suppose Christians can't drive luxury cars, live in big homes, or wear designer clothing. Are Christians supposed to spend their earnings on nothing but the church? I doubt that was God's plan.

Here's where I think the issue really lies: is it okay to change a physical attribute if you're not happy with it? Is it okay to use the science of medicine (God's science, after all) to choose plastic surgery, particularly when the motivation is strictly self-serving? We use the science of medicine and our knowledge of health to burn fat, increase metabolism, delay osteoporosis, maintain healthy teeth and hair—you name it. There's a certain amount of vanity in all of these efforts, to be sure. Aside from being healthy, we want to be strong, look thin, and style silky locks of hair. So, at what point does a lack in self-esteem justify unnecessary surgery?

Does it ever?

Some of the patient biographies from the ABC show put the whole question of body image and self-worth in perspective. One in particular reads: "A resident of Miami, Florida, Dana has always felt out of place in South Beach's world of hard bodies and pretty faces. As an audio engineer, she wants to feel more confident around the beautiful people she works with in the recording industry."[2]

Wow. All that, because the people she worked with were "pretty."

Is there a plastic-surgery line in the sand? In other words, if your teeth are just *too* crooked and your nose is simply *too* hooked, is it then okay?

If God is a God of absolutes, wouldn't He have an opinion on this?

Every time I think I have the freedom to get plastic surgery, I stop short at this bump in the road: "Or does not the potter have a right over the clay, to make from the same lump one vessel for honorable use and another for common use?" (Rom. 9:21 NASB). If I am the clay on the Potter's wheel, do I have a right to tell Him I don't like my shape? I guess I can tell Him anything I want, but that doesn't necessarily mean He's going to bless it—or my ultimate choice.

I just don't know how far my decision to change my looks can go. According to ABC, changing your appearance is like stepping into a fairy tale. And apparently it's easier: "These men and women are given a truly Cinderella-like experience: A real-life fairy tale in which their wishes come true, not just to change their looks, but their lives and destinies."[3]

Can a person really change her destiny with a nose job?

If so, I guess I should have had one years ago.

What do you think?

Love you,

Sarah

Sarah:

Get real! You are thirty and I am fifty-something. If anybody should be taking a little nip and tuck here and there, it should be me—*not* you. Everything you have is still in the same place as when you got it originally. After four kids I, on the other hand, have seen parts of my body do things I could never imagine. And various parts of me have moved to where they never should have gone! And *you* talk about plastic surgery!

Let's begin with the basics. To be cut or not to be cut, that is the question. Do I think getting plastic surgery is a biblical or a cultural issue? Answer: a little of both, which is why this is a most interesting topic. Let's start with the cultural aspect.

We are so image-conscious in this country that we are creating a multimillion-, if not multibillion-, dollar-a-year industry. You stand in the checkout line at the grocery store, after putting your rice cakes on the conveyor belt, and notice the models on the fronts of the women's magazines. These women are all gorgeous and thin and perfect—and honestly, they are the kind you love to hate, or at least dislike intensely. But lately, we have been hearing about all the fix-it jobs the cover designers do on these models. Thin the legs a little more, narrow the waist a bit, thicken the hair—make that which is already beautiful now surreal.

I think it is interesting that even some of the models themselves have started to complain, saying the pictures are not accurate representations of who they are. Actress Kate Winslet said she didn't appreciate the reshaping of her legs on a movie magazine; she said she preferred her real shape. Bigger, but better.

Remember the commotion when Jamie Lee Curtis decided she wanted to be photographed for *More* magazine as she really is? No fancy lighting, no touch-ups, no model's tricks. She said:

> I don't have great thighs. I have very big breasts and a soft, fatty little tummy. And I've got back fat. People assume that I'm walking around in little spaghetti-strap dresses. It's insidious—Glam Jamie, the Perfect Jamie, the great figure, blah, blah, blah. And I don't want the unsuspecting 40-year-old women of the world to think that I've got it going on. It's such a fraud. And I'm the one perpetuating it.[4]

I love this woman! She tried to liberate a body-conscious public from the burden of physical perfection with what she calls her "true thighs" picture. (She was in the movie *True Lies* with Arnold Schwarzenegger. Nice wordplay, huh?) The problem is we continue to buy the *big* lie that if we diet hard enough, get the right clothes, and allow surgeons to refashion our faces, we will have perfect lives. Nothing could be further from the truth. Are you buying into it, my darling?

We can't overlook the role TV plays in all of this. You are so right about the program *Extreme Makeover*. It is sad that over ten thousand people are vying for a shot at a physical redo. How about a program on folks who have undergone plastic surgery and whose lives aren't always dramatically improved? Do they fight less with their spouses? Have they remained faithful to their mates? Can they honestly say they are markedly more at peace inside because they have been so changed on the outside?

Like the citizens of first-century Rome who attended the events at the Coliseum and cried out for "bread and circus," the networks feed us a steady diet of what we cry out for. We can't lay all the blame at the feet of the media when we have indicated so clearly what kind of programming fare we want.

Is there a biblical answer to whether or not plastic surgery is okay? Not directly. This is one of those areas where we have to go to bigger principles. What are those principles?

You mentioned money several times in your letter. You're right. Last time I heard, plastic surgeons weren't doing a whole lot of tummy tucks for free. This is expensive stuff, and unless the surgery is reconstructive and medically justifiable, most patients pay right out of pocket—and they pay a lot. So the question becomes *Can you afford it?* Is the money directed to the surgery being redirected from something else that is a greater priority? Your rent, your food, and yes, your tithe?

You make an interesting point that some might think that if you don't spend money on things related to the church, then all the other stuff you buy must be either ungodly or just plain wrong. We buy food, get cars, pay rent or mortgages, and in the process, like the Proverbs woman, we "[watch] over the affairs of [our] household[s]" (31:27). That's a good thing. Buying stuff in excess, or worshipping at the altar of material gods (which plastic surgery might quickly become) is wrong. *Everything in moderation* is a great biblical standard for living.

I don't see a stated objection to plastic surgery. There are even those circumstances where it truly is necessary: a child born with a cleft palate, someone suffering severe burn injuries. But before anyone diverts the funds and the time to something so clearly involved with self, she has to ask herself, "Why am I doing this?"

Do you think others will like you more? Will you like yourself more? Do you think God will love you more? Don't cluck your tongue. Really, "Why?" is the important first question.

If you can afford it, without taking something away from the family budget that is necessary (because this does not fall in the necessary category), and if doing this is not a placebo for something hurting deep inside, and if you have prayed—

really prayed—about it until you have an answer, then, well . . . We'll do lunch and talk about it some more because I think it is ridiculous for a woman with your beauty even to think about this.

ABC is marketing a big lie. It is not a Cinderella-like transformation. It is a fix-up on the outside without touching the inside. I think Cinderella's stepsisters were uglier on the inside than on the outside. Cinderella was described as good-hearted. If she hadn't been, she would have been just as unattractive as her stepsisters, whether the glass slipper fit her or not.

This really is role reversal. Time is marching all over my face, and *you're* considering plastic surgery? Now, I'm having one of those days.

Love,

your loving and totally confused mother

Mom:

You asked me why. That's the first and most important question, right? Well, I'll answer *you* with a question. Have you ever wondered what it would be like to be physically "perfect"?

I know that sounds like a hopelessly shallow question, but I'm going somewhere with it—trust me.

Do you ever think about the kind of life Elle McPherson (substitute any model's name you wish) leads, and what she thinks when she wakes up in the morning? Does she look in the mirror, make a quick examination, and think *Let's see. Smile: brilliant. Legs: long. Hair: thick. Eyes: enormous. Yep. Still perfect.*

You see, I've wondered all of this at one point or another. And I think what I realized is that when you come right down to it, plastic surgery is a question of satisfaction.

Here's the reason people get plastic surgery—the "why," if you will: because they don't think God gave them "enough."

You tell me I'm beautiful. I can rattle off a hundred retorts (you've heard me do it). I wish I had *more*—more height, more hair, more eyelashes, and, well, *less* weight, anyway. I find myself in running dialogues with God: "Why don't you just let me tell you what I ought to look like? I mean, I'm living in this body, after all. Plus, have *you* ever been a thirty-year-old woman? I just want to be *satisfied* with my looks!" (As an aside, my husband calls this the "moving-target syndrome." Even if God gave me what I wanted, I'd still want *more*. That's sin nature for you).

What I guess I'm forgetting is that God's definition of satisfaction is different from mine (and *definitely* different from the Rolling Stones'): "Satisfy us in the morning with your unfailing love, / that we may sing for joy and be glad all our days . . . With long life will I satisfy him and show him my salvation" (Ps. 91:14, 16).

Unfailing love, joy, and salvation are satisfaction of a different color. Different from long legs, white teeth, and perfect hair, don't you think? Different because of how they last, because that which satisfies most is also that which endures.

Beauty is temporary. Eventually those implants, flat stomachs, and button noses are going right into the ground with everything else. The temporary isn't meant to satisfy—only to preoccupy.

The kind of satisfaction that Christ promises lasts forever.

The women who recognize it, who grasp hold of it, might also be the ones who pass on plastic surgery.

One of my favorite books is *The Princess Bride* (by the same author of the screenplay for *Butch Cassidy and the Sundance Kid*, believe it or not). The book begins with the story of Adela, the most beautiful woman in the world.

As she strolled through the family rose gardens watching the sun rise, she felt happier than she had ever been. "Not only am I perfect," she said to herself, "I am probably the first perfect person in the whole long history of the universe. Not a part of me could stand improving, how lucky I am to be perfect and rich and sought after and young and . . ." Young? . . . "I don't quite see how I'm going to manage to always be young. And when I'm not young, how am I going to stay perfect? And if I'm not perfect, well, what else is there?"[5]

What else, indeed.

Later, we meet Buttercup. She had fallen in love with a young man whom she later learned had been killed at sea. She entered her room to mourn his loss, eventually emerging days later:

[Buttercup] had entered her room as just an impossibly lovely girl. The woman who emerged was a trifle thinner, a great deal wiser, and an ocean sadder. This one understood the nature of pain, and beneath the glory of her features, there was character. . . . She was eighteen, she was the most beautiful woman in a hundred years. She didn't seem to care.[6]

In its own way, this modern fairy tale makes a strong point: beauty isn't all it's cracked up to be. You can either live your life in fear of the dreaded "stomach pooch" or you can live your life—and live it for God.

Perfection, even if you have it, never lasts.

But character endures.

ABC may be telling a big lie with its *Extreme Makeover*. But can you blame it, really? I mean, if the media is not actively seeking significance through God and doesn't perpetuate a life of character, how else can it cater to a lost world but by trying to fill its God-shaped void with temporal pursuits?

I suppose they do it with book clubs and self-help seminars, gurus, and plastic surgery.

Like Adela, if they can't attain perfection, what else is there?

For me and you, plenty.

Or should I say . . . *more*?

Love,

your 100 percent genuine, no aftermarket-product-added daughter

Part 2

Self-Worth

Spinning with the Gingerbread Women

"Everything has got a moral,
if only you can find it."
—LEWIS CARROLL

4

:ᚢ:

Perfectionism and Competition

Mom,

I think I know what it is to love God: "Love the LORD your God with all your heart and with all your soul and with all your strength" (Deut. 6:5). And though I don't always get the gold star on this one, I also know what it is to love others: "Love your neighbor as yourself . . . [this] is more important than all burnt offerings and sacrifices" (Mark 12:33).

But what about me? How do I love . . . me? Me and I have had long conversations, spent tons of quality time together, and lived side by side our whole lives. But for some reason, I just can't seem to figure out how to give me the love she deserves.

Show me a woman who hasn't at some point struggled with her self-esteem, and I'll show you a liar. Whether Christian or non-Christian, black or white, young or old, it seems that feeling inadequate is as universal as bad hair on school picture days. Sometimes we regular people are even lucky enough to catch the beautiful and famous people in rare moments of revelation. Take Jennifer Aniston, for example, who's been quoted as saying: "I feel, half the time, like I am one of these teenage girls . . . feeling stupid, [not] feeling good enough, [not] feeling adequate, asking 'What am I doing?'—it doesn't go away. Coming from a divorced family . . . being overweight . . ."[1]

Now, I can comfortably say I have the tool kit for great self-esteem. I have a relationship with Christ (and that means an eternally secure future), a loving and supportive husband, a circle of encouraging friends, and the unconditional love of my family. But here's the tough part: no matter what I do, or what I'm told, I tend to see myself as falling short.

It's not as if I haven't received a compliment or a "Well done!" in my life. In that regard, I'm a pretty lucky woman. But I'll tell you, it's not the praise or the encouragement I remember. It's the self-appointed mark I didn't hit that always takes the cake.

Self-worth can come from different motivations. Some are good, and some are pretty tyrannical. Mine happens to be perfectionism, or as I like to call it, the "Do it all, do it right, do it the best and twice on Sundays" disease.

Ah yes, the plague of the type-A (and firstborn) personality. You know what I mean—you're one too. We have to do everything right, walk in lockstep, outachieve everyone. We have to cook the best meals, keep the best homes, have the best jobs, lead the most ministries, raise the best kids.

Remember my friend Iris in high school? She's how I first

learned the art and sham of perfectionism. She was beautiful and smart, popular and talented. She was everything I wanted to be, but it was almost as if the starting gun went off the minute we shook hands. Our whole high school careers, we were in a silent race, trying to beat each other to the finish line—to see who could get the longest paragraph of activities and accolades under that senior picture.

I ran that race in college and then in law school. In fact, I'm still running it. And I'm beginning to understand that for better or worse, it's how I usually see worth in myself. I know that because when I win at something, outperform a peer, or overaccomplish a goal, I breathe a little sigh of relief and think, *Whew! Now I can chill out for a while, because I like where I'm at.* But it doesn't last. Pretty soon, I'm back to whipping myself on to the next challenge.

That's the funny thing about perfectionism—it never lets you rest.

So, how do you fight the dragon of perfectionism? And if we're told, "Do your best to present yourself to God as one approved, a workman who does not need to be ashamed" (2 Tim. 2:15), then how much work, how much "doing" is actually enough?

I can't see myself the way God sees me. And even if I did, I still wouldn't see His love for me as sufficient to establish my worth. I need to stand out, be different, be remarkable—be set apart by my achievements. It's why I try so hard to be the best—especially because I serve a God who loves *everyone* and died for *everyone!*

And here is the really crazy, persistent thought: if He gives love so freely, without our having to work for it, then how much is it really worth?

Because I struggle with His love for me, I struggle with loving myself.

So I ask you: how do you love the one person you know best in the world but often dislike the most?

How do you redraw your self-portrait?

Love,

Me

Dear Firstborn:
Or should I call you my Runner? You must be so very tired from all the racing around you've been doing for such a long time, constantly trying to outdistance yourself from someone you think just might perform better than you.

You remind me of the gingerbread man, who said: "You can run and run as fast as you can, but you won't catch me, I'm the gingerbread man."

He was running for his life, and it sounds, in some ways,

as if you are, too. Stop running for a moment, and catch your breath.

Much of what I hear you saying seems to be tied to the idea that your self-worth is a combination of *doing* what you think has to be done (and it better be done better than anyone else), and *adding* in everyone else's opinion of how you did it. Gingerbread woman, that is an exhausting way to live!

My dearest, you forget that the only One you have to please is your heavenly Father—and He is already pleased. Look at the word *Abba*. It translates into the word *Daddy*. It carries with it a sense of connectedness and intimacy. We cannot get closer to Him than through the word *Abba* (See Rom. 8:15).

How amazing that the great Creator of the universe, the one who hung the stars and filled the oceans, gives us the privilege, the permission, and the joy of referring to him as our Daddy. That name frees us to be completely open with Him and reminds us we can trust Him completely. But it also assures us He loves us. Our heavenly Daddy cradles us with everlasting arms of love. Scripture tells us: "He will take great delight in you, / he will quiet you with his love, / he will rejoice over you with singing" (Zeph. 3:17).

Like a tender parent, God sings us a lullaby of love. He watches over us as we travel through the dream of life. And like a strong and protective Parent, He "shields [us] all day long, / and the one the LORD loves rests between his shoulders" (Deut. 33:12).

Does that sound like someone for whom you must perform *or* someone who loves you just because you are His daughter? Far too many of us get the sense that if we have the cleanest house, raise the most obedient kids, have the most perfect marriage, or get the best job, somehow, some way, people will love us, and in turn we will see ourselves as people who are worthy of love.

In truth, that's a hellish formula designed to frustrate us into a sense of failure and depression. Joy is defined as seeing ourselves as He sees us, through His eyes of love.

Remember the verse that says we love Him because "He first loved us" (1 John 4:19)? Can you comprehend, dear one, what that truly means? Before we had the chance to get straight As or win the title of Homecoming Queen, He loved us. Before we were baptized, took Communion, or taught Sunday school class, He loved us. Even after we've been divorced or had an abortion or dabbled in lesbianism, He loves us. There is *no* running here, my daughter. Only resting. With God, it is not about the *doing*, it is about the *being*. We are His. Period. And that profound yet simple truth pours worth and value and significance into our souls. God loves us, and we are and always will be His.

It is not enough for me to list off your accomplishments

(brilliant lawyer, horsewoman extraordinaire, phenomenal vocal musician, and so on) if *you* don't grab hold of His love. If you find self-worth only through striving for perfection and other people's affirmation, then you will always miss the big picture of who you really are: a most beloved daughter of a King.

In the classic tale of "Beauty and the Beast," isn't it easier for most women to relate to Beauty instead of the Beast? But try, for a moment, to step into this story and cast yourself in the part of the Beast.

You are, in a word, a monster. Your fur is matted and full of dirt from the forest where you have been hunting for your dinner. Your long claws prevent you from embracing anything tenderly because you might crush it with your brute strength. Nobody wants to hug a Beast.

Nothing seems to release you from the wretched curse that turned you into a ghoul. It's probably pretty safe to imagine that the Beast's self-worth was negligible. The world saw a monster, but he knew he was different inside. Nobody else could tell.

There have been others who have seen themselves marred by a monstrous condition of sin:

- Isaiah: "Woe to me. I am ruined! For I am a man of unclean lips" (6:5).
- Jeremiah: "I remember my affliction and my wandering, /

the bitterness and the gall. / I well remember them, and my soul is downcast within me" (Lam. 3:19).

- David: "For I know my transgressions, / and my sin is always before me" (Ps. 51:3).
- Paul: "Christ Jesus came into the world to save sinners— of whom I am the worst" (1 Tim. 1:15).
- A Samaritan woman who was being sexually promiscuous (see John 4).
- A woman caught in the very act of sexual immorality (see John 8).

All of these were "beasts" of a kind. The monstrosity of sin could have left them hideous, but as in the fairy tale, all experienced a miraculous transformation.

> "Beast, how you scared me!" she cried. "I never knew how much I loved you until just now, when I feared I was too late to save your life."
>
> "Can you really love such an ugly creature?" asked the Beast faintly. "Beauty, you only came just in time. I was dying because I thought you had forgotten your promise."[2]

Love transformed the Beast into a beloved prince, just as God's love transforms us into His children. He will never forget his promise. He knew we were dying from sin, and He sent the Prince of all princes to die a monstrous death in our place.

Like the Beast, we raise our heads toward heaven and ask, "Can you really love such an ugly creature?" The answer falls gently on our hearts. "Yes," says the King, "and I always will."

Daughter, there is no performance needed here. No constant report card from other people to tell you if you are succeeding or failing. Your self-worth, the value of who you are, comes from the King Himself. He bent down from heaven and said to you, "Beauty, you must not die."

And He transformed you forever.

Mom

Mama:

Matted fur, long talons, brute strength—a fitting description, because there are times we've all felt like Pigpen from the *Peanuts* cartoon instead of the snow queen. In fact, I once read: "Man's greatness lies in his capacity to recognize his wretchedness."[3]

Criminy! I must be one *major* monument to greatness.

I appreciated your analogy to "Beauty and the Beast." Yet it illustrated some things I already recognize.

I know I'm His.

I know He loves me just because I'm His daughter.

I know He loved me before I loved Him, in spite of my monstrosity.

Knowing is not the problem. It's *feeling* that's the real dilemma.

I think opinions are easier to change than heart conditions. I've already been convinced—on that journey of my own spiritual development—of the rightness of what you wrote. But my *feelings* are lagging behind.

You called me your Runner. I run because I want to be set apart. I want to be set apart because I feel that I will be loved more, or differently. After all, the whole problem for me is *feeling* worthy when everyone else in the world is getting the same portion of God's great love. With 6.5 billion people on the earth, it's easy to feel lost in a sea of sameness.

How does one feel distinctive? Sure, God loves me. He loves everyone. So much so that he died for everyone. I certainly wasn't the only name on His heart when He hung on that Roman cross. But does He love me individually—and uniquely? It made me think about what it means to be special in God's sight.

Sitting outside today shed some light on an answer. It's Indian summer here in Maryland, but the leaves have already turned. There isn't a single color duplicated anywhere; on any leaf they are all totally unique. Our dogs chased each other around the yard—different breeds, and totally different personalities, unlike any that have ever been born or will be born.

Then I heard the titter of a chickadee in the pear tree in our front yard, and I remembered reading: "Are not five sparrows sold for two pennies? Yet not one of them is forgotten by God. Indeed, the very hairs of your head are all numbered. Don't be afraid; you are worth more than many sparrows" (Luke 12:6–7).

Sparrows. Hairs. Little things in the universe, but God made them, numbers them, cares for them.

I realized, *I am "God's workmanship"* (Eph. 2:10)!

Remember when you used to laughingly ask, "How can four kids born to the same parents be so completely different from each other?" As an adult, I'm even more reminded of our uniqueness: the tomboy, the scientist, the filmmaker, the writer; blonde, brunette, black-haired; tall, short, courageous, quiet, shy, loud, and every other combination under the sun. If it's that way in our family, how much more so is it in God's family, where we don't all share the same genetics?

He took the time, the creativity, the effort to make every living thing unlike anything else in all His creation. And He did it lovingly, assigning different talents, abilities, appearances, hopes, desires, and futures to all of us so that we might fulfill individual purposes on this planet—do something that no one in all human history has ever done in quite the same way.

God loved me enough not to create me as a clone. That penchant for sweets? Mine. The funky birthmark on my leg? Mine, too. That knack for impersonations, love of the color blue, and dimple under my bottom lip? You guessed it.

That strange and individual combination of things that makes me *me* is the beginning of a foundation for worth.

He wanted me *precisely* as I am.

Oh, and remember Iris? Well, I was thinking about the "race" and our persistent competition, and I thought of 2 Corinthians 10:12: "We do not dare to classify or compare ourselves with some who commend themselves . . . They are not wise." Apparently, using comparison and competition as a means for establishing self-worth isn't a recipe for success after all. That means no whining that someone got better looks or a sharper intellect or more height.

He designed me to be as *I am.*

Not only did He create me as unique, He promises to acknowledge me, recognize me, protect me, remember me: "The Son of Man will also acknowledge him before the angels of God" (Luke 12:8). And " 'Because he loves me,' says the LORD, / 'I will rescue him; / I will protect him, for he acknowledges my name' " (Ps. 91:14).

You don't remember strangers, and you don't protect casual acquaintances. These are *personal* promises. So personal, in fact, that I realize God would have sent His Son to die for me if I were the only person on earth.

So, I'm rather important. I'm set apart after all!

"Thy hands have made me and fashioned me" (Ps. 119:73 KJV). I looked down at my own hands today and studied my fingers. I laughed, thinking, *My fingerprints are incapable of reproduction. How like God to give me a reminder of my uniqueness.* My fingerprints are kind of like His love note, a divine Post-it that never comes off: "I made you like this because I love you so much."

So about that race that we were talking about . . . I guess I hit the yellow tape some time ago.

Love,

Sarah

5

Balancing the Demands of Life

Darling daughter:

When you and your sister were little, you used to love to run around the house, screeching and jumping, whenever you heard the theme song to *Wonder Woman*. Remember that old TV show?

You were crazy about that program, but your sister really thought she *was* Wonder Woman—all she needed were the power bracelets. Grandma, precious lady that she is, helped Rebekah reach her dream by making her a Wonder Woman costume, complete with the bracelets. For the next year, Rebekah flew through the house.

Some of us never seem to outgrow the fantasy, and we still think we can fly through life, doing 150 things at the same time—all perfectly performed, all perfectly on time, and in truth, all perfectly impossible.

You were little when the radical feminists appeared on the

cultural horizon. Their mantra was "You can have it all!" But they didn't finish the sentence, and as a result, many women felt like failures because they weren't having it all.

In truth, you *can* have it all, just not *all* at the same time.

Week after week during my radio broadcasts, I hear women share how they try to juggle all of life's demands. They have jobs outside the home, and they remind me that in some parts of the country, forty hours is a short work-week. They come home to take care of husbands, houses, and children. They try to contribute to some activity at church, wallpaper the bathroom, maintain significant friendships, attend a fantastic women's conference, help with the Christmas cookie exchange, hit the treadmill three times a week, keep up with current events—and, of course, have a meaningful daily quiet time with the Lord.

Who are we kidding? Wonder Woman is a comic book character and the rest of us live in the real world!

We're making ourselves physically ill and getting depressed in greater and greater numbers. Can we even wonder why? There is something much deeper here than women wanting a pair of power bracelets.

I think too often a woman believes she has to do it all because:

- She doesn't know how to say no.
- She thinks if she says no, she is going to disappoint someone.

- She doesn't know how to prioritize tasks.
- She doesn't know how to delegate tasks.
- She has confused the urgent with the important.
- She is afraid if she stops running, she won't be able to handle the stillness.
- She believes God will be displeased with her if she doesn't keep running.

Do you recognize yourself somewhere on this list? If you do, take your superhero cape off and sit awhile.

The Brothers Grimm wrote a strange little tale called "The Three Spinners." It's the story of a peasant girl sent to spin for a queen. Showing the girl three rooms filled to over-flowing with flax, the queen said, "Now you can spin me this flax and when you can show it me all done you shall have my eldest son for bridegroom; you may be poor, but I make nothing of that—your industry is dowry enough."[1]

As you can imagine, the girl began to weep because she knew, even if she lived to be a hundred years old, she could not spin all that flax.

Have you ever felt like the peasant girl, so overwhelmed by the tasks before you that all you can do is sit and weep? Twenty-first-century women are not looking at rooms filled with flax, but we are looking at the many responsibilities of modern life that weigh us down and burn us out.

There is a happy ending to this little fairy tale and a lesson for us as well.

The peasant girl had an encounter with three spinners who passed by the castle. "The first of them had a broad foot, the second had a big under-lip that hung down over her chin, and the third had a remarkably broad thumb."[2]

The three women offered to help spin the flax if they were permitted to sit with the peasant girl at her wedding feast with the prince. As it turned out, each of their physical deformities was well suited to the individual task of spinning flax. The girl agreed, and the women started spinning.

You can guess what happened. In short order, all three rooms of flax were spun into great heaps of yarn and the wedding plans were arranged. The girl kept her promise, and the three spinners went to the wedding and took their places at the head table. The peasant girl found a way to get her job done by sharing the workload, and in so doing she went from weeping to weaving.

Darling, we women live our lives in seasons. There is the season of childhood and adolescence. For many, the dating and courtship season follows. Young married life with children precedes the eventual empty nest. Widowhood is the final season. True, many women stay in a season of singleness or childlessness, but regardless, all of us hear that inner clock ticking that marks the changes occurring in our bodies with the passage of time.

Ask yourself, "What season am I now in? What are my primary responsibilities now—for this time? Are there any tasks I can postpone until the next season? Must I do it all *now*, or can it wait?"

When you and your siblings were little, you recall I did not work outside our home. Raising four little ones, very closely spaced, was more than a full-time job. But outside my door, the radical voices of the day shouted that a woman would find "self-actualization" (their word) only if she worked outside the home. Childhood is fleeting, with memories and magical moments that cannot be repeated. I chose to listen to a still, small voice that whispered the need to nurture my little ones and to look well to the ways of my household.

As I tended to your needs (like when all four of you had chicken pox at the same time—in January, with a record snowfall), I recognized I was in a season. Your granny used to say, "This too shall pass" (it was passing so much faster for her than for me). But it was a season. Not a lifestyle, but a season— filled with *Mister Rogers* and Pampers.

And the season did pass. Eventually, the next season of my life took me to Washington, D.C., where I found myself sitting with the president of the United States at the White House. That's a long way from diapers, but it was the perfectly orchestrated season of my life. And this season will pass, too.

The peasant girl had a season of spinning, but it ended. The Grimm brothers wrote that the three spinners were so ugly—the one with a broad foot from treading, the second with a hanging lip from licking the thread, and the third having a broad thumb from twisting the thread—that the prince declared his new bride should never again touch flax. Goodbye, spinning wheel, hello, throne room.

The lesson in this story is about sharing the load. What one woman couldn't do, four women could. The peasant girl wasn't Wonder Woman, but she got the job done by getting help from others. Don't be afraid to ask for help, my dear one. If you can't do it all—and you probably can't—then get the help you need. God designed us for community, and your asking for some assistance just might be someone else's opportunity to serve.

So, my little spinner, what season are you in? What blessings can you identify that are germane to just this time of life? What challenges are unique to where you are right now? Are you trying to go it alone? Can you stop spinning long enough to write back?

I am anxious to hear from you.

Love,

Mom

P.S. Have you seen my power bracelets?

Dear Mom:

Last night, I came home from a long day at the office and made the coffee and the lunches for tomorrow's workday. Then I emptied the dishwasher, made dinner, started a load of laundry, and wrapped a present for a friend's upcoming baby shower. After that, I returned a few phone calls (to friends with various needs, all apparently urgent), tidied up around the house, and finally fell asleep facedown in the book I was attempting to read.

I don't even have kids yet. But I can't seem to make it past 10:00 PM without collapsing from sheer exhaustion. The alarm buzzed me awake at 6:30 this morning, and all I could think was, "Lord, help me—I'm never gonna make it today!"

So, your list—the reasons a woman thinks she has to do it all? Accurate, and a little . . . intimidating. I mean, without lifting a finger, I plead guilty to:

- not knowing how to say no
- thinking that if I say no, I am going to disappoint someone
- not knowing how to delegate tasks
- confusing the urgent with the important

Here's my biggest struggle, though: I believe God will be displeased with me if I don't keep going, if I don't consistently "get something done."

Why? Well, I guess I feel lazy otherwise.

It makes for a very tired life. In fact, I have trouble even relaxing on vacation. I've been known to tote weighty philosophical tomes as "leisure reading" to the beach, just so I could feel that even if my body wasn't doing anything, I was at least still working my mind. Weekends aren't for relaxing, either—they're for *accomplishing*. Dry cleaning, banking, home renovations, grocery shopping—the list is endless. I justify my constant activity simply because I am convinced the Lord is pleased with a productive life—that through activity and industry, I will be able to fulfill the spiritual model of wife and homemaker.

I've never really been swayed by the siren song of the modern feminist. My attitude is that her priorities are out of whack and she's probably living mostly for herself anyway. But I suppose what I have done, using God's Word as my life's instruction book, is to take Proverbs 31:10–31 to the extreme. I see the "wife of noble character" as a hyperachiever, so I use that as my excuse for overcommitment. In fact, look at what she manages to regularly accomplish:

She selects wool and flax and works with eager hands . . . She gets up while it is still dark; she provides food for her family and portions for her servant girls. She considers a field and buys it;

out of her earnings she plants a vineyard. She sets about her work vigorously; her arms are strong for her tasks. She sees that her trading is profitable, and her lamp does not go out at night . . . She opens her arms to the poor and extends her hands to the needy . . . She makes coverings for her bed; she is clothed in fine linen and purple . . . She watches over the affairs of her household and does not eat the bread of idleness. (PROV. 31:13, 15–18, 20, 22, 27)

This woman is a cook, seamstress, interior decorator, business tycoon, and volunteer, and she apparently *never* succumbs to laziness. In fact, twice in that passage we read she's a hard worker: "She sets about her work vigorously," and she "does not eat the bread of idleness."

I am so impressed. And at the same time, *so* discouraged.

Maybe women needed less sleep three thousand years ago.

I know I'm in a season right now of young, married life. But the fatigue I have as a thirty-year-old working woman gives way to anxiety about what's to come. How will I possibly keep up with kids? How will we be able to stay involved in all their activities? Will we be good parents? Will I be able to keep up with my friends? How will I be able to maintain the house? And then there's carpooling and volunteering at church and the PTA and . . .

Where's my spinning wheel, anyway?

You asked what tasks might be able to wait until another

season. I have trouble answering this question, because everything in my current stage of life feels very pressing, very immediate. The tasks around the house? If the laundry and dishes don't get done, I'll be stinking to the heavens and eating from the dog's bowl. The social commitments? Well, I want to honor my friends and the stages of *their* lives, so hurting them by bowing out isn't in the cards, either. The home renovations? I am just plain tired of living in an unfinished house.

So how do I prioritize? How do I distinguish what can wait?

In case you haven't noticed, I may also have a *bit* of a control problem. Sure, I can delegate some tasks to my husband or my friends. But does that mean I'll be as satisfied with the results as if I had done them myself? Hmmm . . . probably not.

And another thing: I take pride in my husband's recognition of my good "wifery." He compliments my cooking, praises my decorating, commends me on my financial management, thanks me for the careful selection of gifts for his friends and family, and makes me feel all-around as if I've done a good job (frequently when plenty of other people are around to hear it). It feels good. And is it wrong to take pride in his responses? Even more to the point, are my *own* priorities unbalanced if I admit to you (I'll be brutally honest here) that there are times when I've thought, *Yeah, buddy—you've got a good gig here. I keep a pretty tight house. You ought to thank your lucky stars.*

I guess what it comes down to is this: how do you let go enough to rest? How can modern-day women take what looks in Proverbs 31:10 to be a standard of overachievement and realistically apply it to lives that are already overrun with commitment?

All right, that's all I have time to write for now.

I've got some purple to fold.

Love you,

Me

Girlfriend:

You need to stop what you're doing and go out for lunch! You are *way* too stressed for a young woman of only thirty. You have taken the expression "You go, girl!" far too seriously.

Now, would you like some really honest conversation with your mama? Here is my little secret: don't tell anyone, but I do not like that lady portrayed in Proverbs. She had her act together just a little too neatly for me. This woman frustrates me because I will *never* be like her.

Look at this poetic portrait of Miss Perfect:

- She has great character (v. 10).
- She has a husband who adores her because she never embarrasses or hurts him (vv. 11–12).
- She is the Martha Stewart of her day because she loves to work with her hands (v. 13).
- She apparently doesn't need as much sleep as the rest of us (v. 15).
- She obviously finds time to work out at the gym, as evidenced by her toned upper arms (v. 17).
- She is a successful businesswoman (her real estate investment yields a profit) while managing to maintain a cottage industry on the side (vv. 18, 24).
- She clearly loves to work with wool (v. 19).
- She is an interior decorator, using such stylish colors as red and purple (vv. 21–22).
- She has a sense of humor, a keen intellect, and a sharp sense of discernment along with a high level of productivity (vv. 25–27).
- And oh yes, she has perfect children (v. 28).

After reading about this virtuous woman, I need to take a nap. And that puts me in with some mighty good company. After God did all of His creating, the Bible tells us He rested. Let me repeat that: *God rested*. Did it make Him lazy, or somehow less sovereign, that He stopped His work and rested? Clearly not. But there is a message here for us women.

We do not know how to rest. I think I'll start a movement and call it the National Women's Sleep Day. I'll call on businesses, husbands, and children all across the land to let women take a day off and just sleep in. Sounds wonderful, doesn't it?

Sweetie, we don't need a national movement. We already have a role model in Jesus. Have you ever stopped to consider that Jesus could, if He wanted to, have fed more multitudes or healed even more of the disabled or gone on more fishing trips or traveled to more villages? He could have. But He didn't. Why not?

I think it's because it wasn't about the work He was doing. It was really about the work God was doing through Him. For you and me, it isn't about the work we're doing; it's really about the work God is doing in us.

If we are so busy *doing* all the time, we won't build in those times when we can really "be still, and know that [He is] God" (Ps. 46:10). Don't you think God would rather just have us all to Himself sometimes? Cleaning and cooking and washing and gardening and working and shopping, and all those other things on our to-do list, fit in somewhere, sometime. But if activity robs us of our joy, of our first love, then something is out of balance.

So would you rather be a Martha or a Mary? The story told in Luke 10 really speaks to me personally. Being in Washington, D.C., I have a hundred opportunities to do a hundred things a hundred times a day. (All right, so I am exaggerating. But you get the point.) I read in Luke that Jesus, when visiting the house of these two sisters, found only one who was willing to sit at His feet. The other sister was "distracted" (v. 40). Ouch! There was the Savior of the world who had come to pay a visit, and she was distracted! Oh, she had a clean house, and she served a great meal. She was a great hostess, too, no doubt. But she missed the most important thing of all: Jesus.

Like Martha, I get distracted. I often find myself running *for* Jesus rather than running *to* Jesus. You know what happens when I do that? I just get plain tired. You would think all the stuff I do is important, but in truth it is absolutely useless if I am distracted from sitting at Jesus' feet.

My dearest, you do so many things so well. I am very proud of you. But I want to give you permission (as I give myself permission) just to sit and not be distracted. Jesus would rather have your pure heart than a clean kitchen floor. He gently invites you to spend time with Him so He can tell you how much He loves and values you—just because you are you! He wants to speak to you through His letters written with the ink of divine inspiration. Don't be so distracted *doing* that you neglect just *being* in His presence.

Pour yourself a cup of tea, turn off the TV, radio, and your cell phone, put on some quiet praise and worship music, and just listen while the unconditional Lover of your soul tells you about His love for you. Don't pay any attention to the dust on the coffee table. Rather, let Him dust away your fears and polish your heart with His tender mercies.

Jesus told a complaining Martha that her sister Mary had "chosen what is better" (Luke 10:42). I want to be able to do that. I want to make better choices. But sometimes that means I have to make hard decisions, such as saying no when, out of the fear of disappointing someone, it would be so much easier to say yes. I don't want to have so many commitments that I falter in my commitment to Him. Charles Spurgeon said: "In forty years I have not spent fifteen waking minutes without thinking of Jesus."

That's my desire. I want to have Him so close to my heart that I am never distracted.

As for that Proverbs 31 woman, she is really a poem, not a real picture. The acrostic story has twenty-two stanzas, each one introduced by a letter of the Hebrew alphabet and each one containing a separate tribute to this fictitious woman of virtue. She exists to encourage us in our desire to grow closer to God, but sadly she is often misused as a standard of measurement, for which almost all women come up short. Her verbal portrait is meant to encourage, not discourage.

Rest, darling, rest. Enjoy being in His presence and allow yourself the pleasure of sitting at His feet.

I have to dash now, but anytime you want to arise and call me "blessed" is okay with me.

Love you!

Mom

6

※

Handling Your Mistakes and Life's Disappointments

Dear Mom:

I'm a planner. A list-writing, arrangement-making, preparation-loving planner.

I don't like going into a situation blind, and I *certainly* don't like being surprised by an outcome I didn't anticipate. In fact, all the major decisions in my life have been guided by this sense of preparation. I prepared for college in high school, for law school in college, for the workforce in law school. I did the same for buying a house, changing jobs, even getting pets. I haven't made a single major decision without thinking through every possible outcome and developing strategies to deal with each lurking snafu.

After all, if you're certain of the result, it takes away the fear, right?

Funny thing, fear.

We fallen creatures rely a lot on fear: fear of failure, of embarrassment, of disappointment. That's a big one—disappointment.

I think of how crushingly disappointed Job must have felt when—as a man with ten kids, seven thousand sheep, three thousand camels, five hundred oxen, five hundred donkeys, and countless servants—he lost everything: "My days have passed, my plans are shattered, / and so are the desires of my heart" (Job 17:11).

This was a man "blameless" in God's sight (1:1). Of all the test cases for Satan! Every time I read this story, I think, *Poor Job! Could God have maybe offered up one of the lying tax collectors of Uz? You know—good but not too good? Goes to synagogue faithfully but maybe lied to the rabbi or cheated the offering box a few times. What's a man to think if he's been blameless his whole life and the Lord releases Satan on him?*

Job's discouragement is palpable, and we've all felt it at one point or another: "Where then is my hope? / Who can see any hope for me?" (17:15).

It started me thinking: when you've carefully laid your plans and spun the fabric of all your dreams, how do you deal with the disappointment of shattered hopes?

And if you're not blameless like Job (who is?), what do you do if your own mistakes have caused the shattering? If you've caught an STD because of promiscuous sex, if your abortion has prevented you from having children, if you've made a slew of poor financial decisions or taken a wrong turn when parenting that prodigal kid, how do you get past the feeling that you've single-handedly destroyed your own life?

I love fairy tales, in part because of their neat and tidy happy endings. In fact, you rarely hear a fairy tale begin this way: "When misfortune is after someone, that person may try to hide in all sorts of places or flee into the open fields, but misfortune will still know where to find him."[1]

In the Brothers Grimm tale "Misfortune," the tale gets worse: "Once upon a time there was a man who had become so poor he did not even have a log of wood to keep the fire going on his hearth."[2] This poor man went in search of some wood, finding all the trees were too big for him to manage. When he finally found one of the right size, he was attacked by a pack of wolves. He ran for his life toward a bridge that spanned a rushing river only to discover the bridge was unsound; it collapsed just as he stepped on it. With the wolves at his heels, he jumped into the water but sank to the bottom because he couldn't swim.

Luckily (or so we think), a few fishermen saw the ordeal unfolding and rescued the poor man from the waves. After pulling him from the water, they propped him up against a wall on shore so he could regain his strength. Just as the man came to and began to thank the fishermen, the wall against which he was resting fell on him and killed him.[3]

I think this story redefines *bad day*.

Here's what strikes me the most about this sad tale: its abject hopelessness. That, and the fact that this man appears to have done nothing wrong. He was simply looking for some wood so he wouldn't freeze to death. Was it fair that he was brought to such an end?

I know we Christians have a hope that this poor man didn't—the promise of eternal security from a loving Creator, who reminds us, "For I know the plans I have for you . . . plans to prosper you and not to harm you, plans to give you hope and a future" (Jer. 29:11).

I know the Lord has plans for my life.

But what about *my* plans?

It calls into question what happens when you hope for good, and evil comes, or you look for light, and you're met with darkness (Job 30:26). How do we as Christians deal with that kind of disappointment? And for those of us who have been burned by past letdowns, how do we prevent ourselves from living in *fear* of being disappointed?

If the Lord's plans are already laid out for our lives, what is the point of "hop[ing] for what we do not yet have" and "wait[ing] for it patiently" (Rom. 8:25)?

It's not really up to us anyway . . . is it?

Love,

Me

✧

Dear honest daughter:

I so appreciate the openness of your letter because, truth be told, there is not a one of us who has not experienced disappointment and wondered, *Where was God when I needed Him?*

Here's a news flash (and you better brace yourself): life is full of disappointments. Now, you may pick yourself up off the floor and keep reading. Look at the facts:

Fact: We no longer live in the Garden of Eden.

Fact: Mankind and womankind walked out of Paradise into a sin-sick world filled with temptations, disease, and death.

Fact: We *will* experience Edenesque perfection again, but only when we are spending eternity with Jesus.

So, how do we live with disappointments from now until then?

I am glad you referenced the story of Job. It really is an amazing tale because it addresses the issue of disappointment and suffering by calling into account the question of whether or not God can be trusted. It also speaks of the refining that takes places through troubled times.

Listen to the conversation between God and Satan. Not too many of these are recorded in Scripture, so it must be significant that we are allowed the privilege of hearing that dialogue. Twice God asked of Satan, "Where have you come from?" and twice Satan replied, "From roaming through the earth and going back and forth in it" (Job 1:7; 2:2). Honey, that means that nasty old devil is looking for a way to mess us up. He really hates God, and he hates His children, too.

One of the most effective ways Satan has of causing us to flounder spiritually and emotionally is to have us question God—to tear down that bridge of trust between our Creator and ourselves. When disappointments come, the great Deceiver loves to rattle his tail and whisper into our hearts, "Where was God when you needed Him the most?"

Let me offer a word of caution at this point: we must be careful not to confuse God with a bad decision on our part. I remember Jill Briscoe, one of my favorite Bible teachers, saying once when I interviewed her on my radio show that we need to be careful not to get life and God confused. Gambling away your paycheck, engaging in risky sexual behavior outside of marriage, or having an abortion are all indicators that we do have the liberty to make bad decisions—often with very painful consequences—not evidence that God doesn't care. The powerful promise for those who have stumbled and fallen is the assurance that there is not one bad decision ever made that wasn't paid for at Calvary.

Now, go back to the story of Job. Here was a man whose life spelled s-u-c-c-e-s-s. His 401K was solid, his portfolio was diverse with multiple shares in livestock, and his large family was the picture of perfection. They even loved to party together on a regular basis.

But he experienced a dramatic turn of events when God allowed him to be tested.

Now *there* is a sobering thought: God tests us. Why? Is He some sort of cosmic professor who wants to know how his puny little creatures respond to hostile conditions? Or does God test us so He can reveal His unshakable love for us while assuring us, yet another time, that He can be trusted? The testing is part of the transforming. I heard someone say once that a Christian is like a teabag: She's not worth much until she's been through some hot water!

Testing and transforming go hand in hand. As we walk with God, His desire for us is to be conformed and trans-formed to the image of Christ (see Rom. 12:1–2). For most of us, being transformed is okay if you are cleaning fire-places and a visit from your fairy godmother transforms you from a scullery maid into the prince's heartthrob, complete with glass slipper. But being transformed by being ham-mered on the anvil of God's love is quite another matter.

When Joni Eareckson jumped into the Chesapeake Bay on a hot summer's day shortly after high school graduation, she had no idea her entire life would be radically transformed. That afternoon she broke her neck. She is wheelchair-bound to this day. It would have been easy to say that God aban-doned her, that her life was now defined by hopelessness and all *her* dreams were dashed. But God had other dreams for her—dreams to be lived from the confines of that wheel-chair.

As the president and founder of Joni and Friends, she has encouraged the disabled to see themselves as people of value. She has fought for and testified before Congress on legislation that protects all life—from the preborn to the elderly. Joni's artwork, created by holding a paintbrush in her mouth, has inspired awe and reverence for the world around us. She has sent wheelchairs to people around the world who were pre-viously bound to their beds. Joni and her husband, Ken Tada, have traveled globally to share the love of God. She will never know how many lives she has touched until she is standing (and she *will* be standing) before the throne of grace.

Every time I have interviewed Joni, I am always moved by the calm she exudes—a peace that comes from knowing the everlasting arms of love that lift her daily out of her wheel-chair. My conversations with her always leave me wanting to trust God more.

But what about Joni's plans? Is it fair that she has spent the majority of her life in a wheelchair? The issue isn't fairness. Matthew 5:45 tells us the "rain" (bad times) falls on the just and the unjust. The issue is surrender. Are we willing to trust God enough to say, "Lord, I want your plans to be my plans; whatever comes my way, I trust You"? We can trust Him be-cause God will never disappoint us.

Job's story ends by God blessing "the latter part of [his] life more than the first" (42:12). His flocks of sheep, camels, oxen, and donkeys doubled in size. His new daughters were the most beautiful in the land, and they even received an inheritance (which didn't happen very often in those male-dominated days). In short, his life became better than before his time of testing. Why? Because Job had gone through hell and back by learning to trust God.

I am sure Job never forgot the pain of losing his family. Like broken china, a broken heart always bears a scar. But I think the story of Job tells us that this tested man who loved God was able to appreciate the latter blessings from God because he didn't get bogged down in bitterness over broken dreams and disappointments.

So, my darling, the really unfortunate part of the Grimms' tale "Misfortune" is that the man in the story seemed to be wandering aimlessly. We who know and love God don't have to wander. We have to surrender—and trust. There is a wise saying: "When you cannot see the hand of God, learn to trust the heart of God."

Before she died, Madame Chiang Kai-shek turned from being a Communist to becoming a Christian. She lived in a nation filled with dashed dreams and constant disappointments. Yet in the midst of a cultural revolution, she found the peace of knowing God:

In traditional Chinese painting, there is just one outstanding object, perhaps a flower. Everything else in the picture is subordinate. An integrated life is like that. What is that one flower? As I see it now, it is the will of God. I used to pray that God would do this or that; now I pray that God will make His will known to me.[4]

What a wonderful way to avoid disappointment! May God's dream for your life be your dream. In that, there is no misfortune.

Love,

Mom

Mom:

Remember my good friend Rachel? The one with the infectious laugh and off-the-wall sense of humor? About a year ago, she learned she was pregnant and was overjoyed. At the fourth month, a heartbeat couldn't be found, but her OB-GYN assured her it was nothing to be concerned about—that the baby had possibly shifted and its heartbeat was out of range. But at the fifth month, further testing revealed that the baby had indeed died and she had been carrying a dead baby for some months.

Rachel loves the Lord and is one of the sweetest spirits I have ever met. She took the painful news with definite grace, clinging to Proverbs 19:21: "Many are the plans in a man's heart, / but it is the LORD's purpose that prevails."

Hmm. My plans are nice, but life is really about God's plans after all.

If I could choke this one down, I think I'd save myself a lot of misery.

What I realized after reading your letter was that it's not that my plans are insignificant, it's just that they don't stem from omniscience or omnipotence. In other words, the Lord delights in giving us what we ask of Him, but only if it's part of His plan for our lives . . . and it might not be. Only He can determine what is in our best interests, even when we're sure we know what is.

I have to tell you another Brothers Grimm tale that surprised me. As oddly dark and hopeless as "Misfortune" was, "The Little Old Lady" turns the tables by putting a fine point on God's purposes for our lives in a seemingly purposeless world (albeit in a rather gruesome way).

The tale centers around an old woman, alone and at the end of her life. She had lost her husband, her two children, all her relatives, and at the story's start, her last living friend. She was bitter and blamed God for her unhappiness, particularly for the death of her sons. But when she heard the tolling of the church bells, she picked herself up and made her way to worship.

I have to admire a woman like this, who, even though she is shaking her fist at heaven, still manages to get up and go to church—almost as if she's saying, "All right, fine! You win."

When she arrived at the church, all the seats were occupied. Looking around, she realized that the occupants of the pews were all her dead relatives and friends, one of whom said, "Look up at the altar, and there you will see your sons." There, on the altar, the old woman saw her two sons: one hanging from a gallows, the other, crushed under the wheel of a wagon. She was told, "That's what would have happened to them if they had lived longer."

And then the little old lady did a funny thing. She went home and thanked God on her knees for "having shown her more kindness than she had been able to understand."[5]

She *thanked God* because she realized He protected her sons. In doing so, He protected her.

Your letter reminded me that we are tested. And while I admit I strongly dislike the concept of being tested (I swore the bar exam would be the last time!), what I realized after reading this tale was that beyond God's proving Himself trustworthy, and beyond His testing us so He can transform us, He often diverts our desires and arrests our plans to protect us.

Now *this* is a concept I like.

"In his heart a man plans his course, / but the LORD determines his steps" (Prov. 16:9).

Our plans are nice. Often we even make them under the auspices of pursuing God's plans and furthering the kingdom. But while we usually feel as if we rule our own lives (choosing where to live, where to go to school, what to do for a living, and whom to marry), those of us who are Christians know better. The Lord gives us the freedom to enjoy our lives, make our plans, pursue our dreams. But He also knows better, and as our divine Dad, He reserves for Himself the power and the right to guide us to the best, rather than the second best.

Sometimes it is easy to imagine what our lives' personal best would look like: health, wealth, security, longevity, happiness. Sometimes the actual best for us means a job interview that didn't pan out, a stillborn child, bankruptcy, or the death of a loved one.

Some real honesty here: I struggle against the fact that God has a cosmic override button in my life. Why? Because I'm selfish, and I have a problem with surrender. Well, that and I'm a control freak.

So, until I better grasp the concepts of testing, transforming, and trusting, I take solace in this: He loves me enough to sometimes protect me from what I want: "But the plans of the LORD stand firm forever, / the purposes of his heart through all generations" (Ps. 33:11).

If He loved me enough to die for me, then the plans and purposes of His heart can't possibly be bad.

Plus, I really didn't want that job in Washington anyway.
Right?

Love,

your daughter

Part 3

Relationships

Sugar and Spice, Not Everything's Nice

"The heart of Christianity is a myth
which is also a fact."

—C. S. LEWIS

7

Marriage

Dear Mama:

I thought I was prepared for marriage. Matt and I were in our late twenties when we married; we had steady jobs and were, in our estimation, older, wiser, and more mature than many of our friends when they got engaged. We had taken pre-marital classes, read books on the marriage relationship, and spent time with a mentor couple just so we could learn the ropes. We were ready to go, convinced our marriage would be perfect.

Nothing in the world could have prepared me for the roller coaster I was to encounter.

As long as I've started with an amusement-park metaphor, let me use another: marriage is like Disney World. Sometimes the day is perfect: the sun is shining, the lines are short, the food is good, and the vendors are as cheerful as Steamboat Willie. And you think, *Wow! I'm at Disney World! This is the greatest day of my life!*

On other days, it's raining so hard you've got standing

water in your Keds, and you have to wait in line forty-five minutes for Space Mountain (or worse, for the bathroom). The hot dogs are cold, and all you really want to do is go back to your hotel room and sleep. But you still think, *Well, I'm at Disney World. And even though this day hasn't been the greatest, I still love it here.*

For me, marriage has been kind of like that. My worst day married is better than my best day single. The support and encouragement I receive, the security and unconditional love, help me daily to understand why some have called marriage the best exercise to understand and practice the love of God.

I have to admit that marriage isn't theme-park perfect by any stretch. No surprise there, considering Paul made a point of recognizing that: "Those who marry will face many troubles in this life, and I want to spare you this" (1 Cor. 7:28).

Paul may have been a fly on the wall during our first six months of marriage. I didn't think it was humanly possible to fight that much.

One of the things Matt and I fought about during those early months was the time we spent together. Matt jokes that I don't just want quality time, but quantity time too. There may be some truth to that. Matt is the one person on earth with whom I cannot spend enough time. But not so for him. What I quickly learned was that in addition to "us" time, he needed "me" time. He needed to come home and veg out for a while in front of the TV after work, to talk to his guy friends on the phone, to write his plays for the Saturday flag-football game, to play his fantasy sports.

Ah yes, fantasy sports—the bane of a young wife's existence. Whether it's football, baseball, basketball, or NASCAR, it's just another aspect of who he is that I don't understand. In fact, it's an interest of his in which I take *no* interest. That brings me to this question: do I have to? Can I just support without taking part? And how much do I have to support? I didn't imagine Matt would give up his interests the minute we were pronounced man and wife (or give them up at all, for that matter), but I didn't think they'd be such a source of contention, either. What do I do when I start to resent what he does (whether work *or* play) because it takes away from the time we could be spending together?

Another time bomb? Taking Matt's last name. Now, I always expected I would take my husband's surname. That's what Christian women do, right? But after we were married, I had plenty of time waiting in line at the DMV, the Social Security office, and the courthouse to think: was I losing a part of myself? I grew up with so many Sarahs in high school that my last name became my nickname. If I took Matt's name, I wouldn't be "Parshall" anymore. Also, like a lot of women these days, I had built a career on my maiden name—all my licenses (including my license to practice law) bear my maiden name. Isn't taking a new name like starting over?

What happened to who I was before? I was a part of *your fam-ily*—our family—not his. And who said I had to take his last name, anyway?

I guess that kind of goes to a bigger issue: submission. I'm a little headstrong. Maybe you've noticed?

Look, I know what it says in Ephesians 5:22–24: "Wives, submit to your husbands as to the Lord. For the husband is the head of the wife as Christ is the head of the church, his body, of which he is the Savior. Now as the church submits to Christ, so also wives should submit to their husbands in everything."

But what if you *know* your husband's about to make a major mistake? Doesn't that verse, if taken to extremes, mean that you're going to be a doormat for the rest of your life? It seems like today's Christian woman has the short end of the stick: her entire youth, she's under the authority of her parents. Then, when she's finally old enough to get out and get married, she finds herself under the authority of her husband! Did God really think a woman needed to be cor-ralled like a wild horse?

And while I'm playing devil's advocate here, let me also point out that the latter portion of Ephesians 5 commands that "husbands ought to love their wives as their own bodies. He who loves his wife loves himself" (5:28). But what if you *know* your husband isn't giving you that kind of love? I've never met a husband who plays by God's rules all the time—particularly as those rules relate to his wife. Are you still required to bend in submission, even if your husband's being a pigheaded oaf?

I guess I already know your answer, but I'm telling you right now, I don't have to like it.

Well . . . maybe I do. And that's where things really get tough.

I sometimes wonder what God could possibly have been thinking when He put two very dissimilar creatures on the earth together and commanded, "The two shall become one." Did Eve chase Adam around the garden, complaining he was too busy naming animals to talk about their future? Did Adam roll his eyes when Eve uprooted his perfectly good hibiscus on the south lawn for bougainvillea just because it matched her color scheme?

Was she emotional and communicative? Was he process-oriented and analytical? If they were so different (and I suspect they were—I mean, they were the prototypes for all husbands and wives to follow), did God really know what He was doing? If so, why in the world would He have permitted those differences to be the sources of such conflict between husbands and wives?

I'm not the only one who thinks this, right?

Surely, other wives—good wives, wives who love their husbands—unconditionally think this kind of thing, too . . . right?

Reassure me, please.

Love,
Mrs. Used-to-Be-Parshall

Dear married daughter of mine:
Welcome to one of the mysteries of marriage. Wives through the ages have learned that somewhere along love's highway, each of us must lose some of *me* while creating this union of *we*.

One very symbolic way of letting society know this union has been formed, in our culture, is for the wife to take her husband's last name. Jesus explained in Matthew that "'a man will leave his father and mother and be united to his wife, and the two will become one flesh.' . . . So they are no longer two, but one" (19:5–6).

It seems to me that when a husband and wife transform themselves from *you* and *me* into *we*, this brand-new family is clearly recognized by one name—the *same* name. I have a hard time accepting the concept of wives keeping their maiden names when they marry, as it looks so much more like *me* than *we* to me.

I loved taking your daddy's last name. Of course I was proud of my maiden name. It represented the family I was born into, the heritage of my family tree, the bloodline from which I came. I will always be my parents' daughter—always. But on my wedding day, I became something else. I was then someone's wife. A few years later, another role was added to my life. I became your mother—and I always will be. And so goes the cycle of life. We go from role to role to role, each one adding to our lives and enriching who we are.

Each role, my darling, adds to us as women. We don't lose anything when we change roles; we merely transition from one life experience to another. Each role adds to the knowledge we have of ourselves and where we fit into God's plan.

You loved fuzzy caterpillars when you were little. You'd hold a little critter on your finger and studiously gazed at its multiple legs while wondering how a bug could be so soft. But some caterpillars, like some women, are designed to change roles. Certain caterpillars metamorphose into butterflies. They spread their wings and experience life from a new perspective.

Being a butterfly doesn't mean the insect wasn't once a caterpillar.

Being a wife does not mean you were not once a daughter or a single woman who had accomplished so very much. This new role, the one that is so identifiable by your new last name, lets you learn not only what it means to be loved, but also how *to* love—and to forgive.

Ruth Bell Graham said that "a good marriage is the union of two forgivers." When your husband is sometimes thoughtless (just as you will sometimes be thoughtless), forgive him. When he acts selfishly (as you will sometimes be selfish), forgive him. When he is occasionally more interested in his world (as you will sometimes be more interested in your world than his), forgive him. Someone once said that success in marriage is not only about *finding* the right mate, it is also about *being* the right mate.

I think we wives can learn an important lesson from a very familiar fairy tale.

> There once lived a Prince who wished more than anything to find a princess to marry. He traveled far and wide, and although he met many princesses, none of them was quite what he wanted. Some were too stout, some were too tall, some were too serious, and some were too silly. Not one of them was everything a real princess should be. And so the sad prince returned home.[1]

This little story continues by telling us that a rain-soaked maiden showed up one dark and stormy night at the palace door, announcing that she was a princess. The girl was muddy with torn clothes and water pouring out of her heels—not exactly what one expected when looking for a princess. But the lass insisted she was one.

The potential mother-in-law (there's the mom, meddling again!) came up with a test to determine if the girl really was a princess. She secretly placed a pea under one mattress, added nineteen more mattresses on top, and then threw on twenty eiderdown quilts for good measure.

We all know what happened. The next morning the queen asked the girl how she slept. She replied: "Very badly indeed. I don't know what could have been in that bed, but it was very hard and uncomfortable! I'm black and blue all over! It's terrible!"[2]

Everyone in the palace then knew she was a real princess—because only a *real* princess could feel a pea through all those mattresses and quilts. And you guessed it: the prince chose her as his wife!

We are never really given an explanation as to why a real princess could feel a pea through all that bedding, so let me venture a guess. I think we real-life princesses are designed to have great sensitivity—a kind of compassion and gentleness that is reflective of who we are as women made in the image of Christ. So many times in Scripture we read of God's "tender" mercies or His "unfailing" compassions. That spiritual sensitivity is a hallmark of a mature believer who truly desires to be like Jesus. Don't you want to be like Him? If you say yes, then let me boldly take the next step and use that dreaded and terribly misapplied and misunderstood word: *submission*.

I thought it was hysterical when the *New York Times* tried to make a story out of a resolution passed one year by the Southern Baptist Convention at one of its annual meetings.

The attendees wanted to reaffirm boldly what the Bible says about the roles of men and women in marriage. So they merely restated, in a resolution, what Ephesians 5 says about the relationship and responsibilities of husbands and wives. Yes, part of that passage *does* say wives should submit to their husbands. The *Times* reported only that part of the vote, recklessly trying to position the resolution as some sort of Neanderthal throwback to times when women walked, head down, five paces behind their men.

But the Old Gray Lady, as the *New York Times* is sometimes called, neglected to point out the rest of the resolution: what the husband's job is, according to Scripture. Men are to "love their wives as their own bodies" (Eph. 5:28). Paul pointed out that no one hates his own body but cares for it, just as Christ cares for the church.

William Barclay said:

Even after he has stressed the subordination of women, Paul goes on to stress even more directly the essential partnership of man and woman. Neither can live without the other. If there be subordination it is not for the sake of subordination but that the partnership may be more fruitful and more lovely for both.[3]

The *New York Times* missed the point. The idea for women is not some sort of servitude but rather a spirit of service. We, like Christ, serve out of love. But honestly, darling, husbands have the much tougher job. They are to love us as Christ loved the church: selflessly, patiently, carefully, lovingly, sacrificially, and unceasingly. There must be one that is the ultimate authority in the home, and that one is the husband. Why? Because God said so, and for a very good reason. As Christ is head of the church, so our husbands are to be the heads of our households. But their God-given authority comes with the mandate to lead like Jesus. What happens when our husbands fail on the job? You guessed it, honey: we forgive!

I like what author Matthew Henry said on the relationship between husbands and wives: "Eve was not taken out of Adam's head to top him, neither out of his feet to be trampled on by him, but out of his side to be equal with him, under his arm to be protected by him, near his heart to be loved by him."[4]

So, my daughter, you are a wife. I pray you will always be sensitive, like the princess in the fairy tale, to your husband's needs, yes, but even more sensitive to what God is doing through you in your role as a wife. Falling in love is the easy part. Growing in love is where the real work is done.

I think I will close this letter with a little Ogden Nash. Think about his wise words when you climb into bed tonight—on top of twenty mattresses and twenty eiderdown quilts:

To keep your marriage brimming,
With love in the loving cup,
Whenever you're wrong, admit it,
Whenever you're right, shut up.[5]

I love you, my daughter.
Mom

Dear old married lady:
First off, I will agree with your views on the value of taking
Matt's name, the duty to forgive and daily grow in love, and
yes, even submit (though the way that phrase has been taken
out of context turns my stomach, too). But I'm still mystified
about the fundamental differences between men and women
in the first place—the same differences that are the source of
so much difficulty, so many arguments, in marriage.

Why are two totally different beings allegedly the perfect
love match?

Look, I know my marriage Bible verses—and what they
say in Matthew, Ephesians, and 1 Corinthians. But these pas-
sages rely on the premise that men and women are similar—
when in my opinion, nothing could be further from the
truth.

Forget John Gray's theory that men are from Mars and women are from Venus. I don't think we're even in the same solar system.

We aren't physically the same: women are smaller, with shorter skeletal structures, fewer red blood cells, larger stomachs, and smaller lungs (strange but true). We aren't emotionally the same: women need affection, conversation, and support; men need sex, recreational companionship, and respect. And we aren't spiritually the same: she submits, he leads; he provides financial support, she tends to the home; he's the head of the house, she's the "weaker partner" (Eph. 5:22-30, 1 Pet. 3:7).

In fact, as long as you've offered some quotes on the subject, I'll trade one myself. Here's what the English writer J. B. Priestley said:

[Women] remain more personal in their interests and less concerned with abstractions than men on the same level of intelligence and culture. While you are briskly and happily generalizing, making judgments on this and that, and forgetting for the time being yourself and all your concerns, they are brooding over the particular and personal application and are wondering what hidden motive, what secret desire, what stifled memory of joy or hurt, are there prompting your thought.[6]

Ha! Personal, brooding, hidden—you see? We don't even *think* the same! Why would God put two of His most dissimilar creatures together in a love match? I don't want to doubt the Almighty, but lately . . . I've had some doubts.

When I've questioned Him in the past, I've learned to remember the one thing that always encourages me, that helps me in "my unbelief" (Mark 9:24): God knows better than we do.

You quoted Matthew 19:5–6 to remind me that when a man and a woman marry, they are no longer two, but one. The passage actually begins with Jesus reminding the Pharisees that "at the beginning the Creator 'made them male and female'" (19:4). In so many words, Jesus was offering a succinct reminder that He made them different, and He did so deliberately. He then went on to explain in the following verses that God also made those different creatures for each other.

Deuteronomy 32:6 says: "Is he not your Father, your Creator, / who made you and formed you?" He made and formed both of us—men and women, Adam and Eve, Matt and me. It stands to reason He would have known what (or *who*) would work together and what wouldn't.

I just love this verse from Isaiah:

> *Do you not know?*
> *Have you not heard?*
> *The L*ord *is the everlasting God,*

the Creator of the ends of the earth.
He will not grow tired or weary,
and his understanding no one can fathom. (40:28)

When it says no one can fathom his understanding, I suppose it kind of puts to rest the idea that He was just plain wrong in pairing men and women in marriage.

I think what's happened is that I've heard for too many years about the "battle of the sexes." Hearing the culture around me repeat that phrase since adolescence has given me the tendency to think about Matt (and men in general, for that matter) from an adversarial perspective. But at some point in time men and women got along just perfectly.

That would be *before* the forbidden fruit.

And the snake.

And what must have been the biggest marriage blowout in history.

I suppose the Fall had the same effect on marriage as it did on everything else in the world: it pitted the participants against each other, and it gave them the same sin-sickness that starts all those arguments I've been wondering about.

The Fall separated what God always designed to be perfectly aligned.

So, knowing we're different, separate, and often totally at odds, maybe the key to harmony is this: "Husbands, in the same way be considerate as you live with your wives, and treat them with respect" (1 Pet. 3:7).

The Greek in that passage literally reads, "Dwell with them according to knowledge." It seems the only way to live with a wife or a husband in an understanding way is to try to really "know" him or her. That means embracing the differences I pointed out, not using them as a springboard for a fight.

Yes, Matt needs "me" time, and yes, he loves his fantasy sports. But I have my own needs: to be cherished, shown affection, and communicated with. Maybe knowing that we're different and recognizing the best, the godliest, way to approach those differences is what God intended all along.

Like forgiveness (that's always, I guess, the godly way to bridge the differences between Matt and me, and to prevent a fight). You reminded me that when Matt's thoughtless, when he's selfish, when he's more interested in his world than mine, to forgive. That kind of reminder to forgive is good when it comes from your mom but even better when it comes from the Bible (and with God's promise of improved behavior, too!): "You wives, be submissive to your own husbands *so that even if any of them are disobedient to the word, they may be won without a word by the behavior of their wives*, as they observe your chaste and respectful behavior" (1 Pet. 3:1–2 NASB, emphasis mine).

So as for those disobedient husbands who might not present the perfect formula for wifely submission, I guess the Lord knew that instead of words, holy living was going to be the only way to get through to the "pigheaded oaf" I talked about in my last letter (gee—ironic that God gives that command to women, who are the more verbal creatures. Who'd have thought?).

I know men and women are different, but by trusting God's Word to be true and His plans to be better than mine, I also know we were created *for* one another. I know, too, that the only way Matt and I are going to survive the next sixty-odd years is by learning to be quick with an apology and ready with God's model of behavior.

And isn't it those differences, those delightful oddities and complexities we have as men and women, that attract us to each other in the first place? We've all heard the old adage, "Opposites attract." Well, while we don't know much about the prince in "The Princess and the Pea," I can almost bet he didn't sleep on twenty eiderdown mattresses and quilts. In fact, he was probably happy with a simple straw mat (typical). But that lovely creature with the rain-soaked hair and sensitive skin was exactly who he wanted because she was everything he wasn't.

Now that I think about it, as different as we are, God sees us as similar because He reconciles us: "There is neither Jew nor Greek, slave nor free, male nor female, for you are all one in Christ Jesus" (Gal. 3:28).

Being created, loved, and owned by the same God means that although we are different, our differences can actually be a gift . . . *not* a curse.

Except for that not-putting-down-the-toilet-seat thing. I'm never gonna understand that one.

Love,

Sarah

8

Children

Dear daughter:

There is a wonderful word: *daughter*. That is the word that changed me forever.

You, my darling, made me a mother. You are my firstborn. And as such, you took me from being a wife, a sister, and a daughter myself and turned me into a mother. In some respects, *that* is the ultimate fairy tale.

When I was little, I loved playing with dolls, just like thousands of other little girls since time began. Something in us has programmed us for that time when we will not only carry life but nurture, imprint, and train up a life—one that we ourselves ultimately must surrender to the Life-Giver Himself. We merely have the privilege of carrying life and raising it according to God's perfect plan.

How wonderfully ironic! God entrusts these perfect little beings into the hands of totally imperfect people and commands us to try to raise them as close to perfection as possible. Impossible! I am so glad God knows how imperfect parents are—how quickly He desires to fill in the gaps when we make mistakes.

Nothing has ever impacted my prayer life like being pregnant. Oh, I watched what I ate, took the multivitamins, and got plenty of rest. But in reality, pregnancy was completely and totally out of my hands. I prayed the prayer of Hannah over and over again: "For this child I prayed; and the LORD hath given me my petition which I have asked of him" (1 Sam. 1:27 KJV).

I knew the outcome of my pregnancy rested in God's gentle hands of perfection and protection. I had to surrender my will to His. I had to be willing to accept what He had planned for me—including whether I would ever bear a child or not.

Isn't it funny how many fairy tales begin with the concept of wanting a child? For example, one very famous tale begins:

> One winter day, when snowflakes were falling, a queen sat at her open bedroom window sewing a tapestry on a frame made of black ebony. She accidentally pricked her finger with the needle, and three drops of blood fell upon the snow. The red drops looked so beautiful against the white snow that she said, "I wish I might have a child as white as snow, red as blood, and as black as ebony."[1]

It is the tale of Snow White, a story that starts with a woman longing for the experience of motherhood. That longing, I believe, is direct evidence of the fingerprints of God in our hearts.

I think God has a profound reason for wooing us to parenthood. As parents, we learn how to practice patience, how to enact appropriate discipline for the purpose of character building, how to forgive with tender mercy, and most important, how to love unconditionally. In other words, we discover what God does for us, *His* children.

In my own experience, being a parent exposed my personal flaws. I have had to learn when it is time to listen and when it is time to speak (and I often get those two mixed up). I have also learned that the "fruit of the Spirit" must be present in my home. It matters little if all that fruit is on display out there in the world somewhere, but it's only rotten apples and sour grapes at home.

I also know my children don't care to listen to lecture after lecture regarding God's principles and His precepts if they don't see them in my life first. That whole "walk the walk, don't just talk the talk" thing is so true. Children want to see truth in our lives, because they must first *see* it if they are to *believe* in it.

By the way, I should let you know, there is no such thing as a perfect parent! Every parent since the beginning of time has blown it. I tell you that so you understand that parenting is tough stuff. We can't do it all by ourselves. But we can do it with God's grace, His wisdom, and His love.

Now that you have told your daddy and me the outstanding news every parent of a married adult child loves to hear, what are your thoughts as you wait for the arrival of your first child?

What advice would you like to hear from your mama? What can I do to prepare you for the most amazing, frightening, daunting, and thrilling experience you will ever have?

I welcome you, along with all the mothers of the world who have gone before you, into a group of women who know firsthand what it means to be present at the formation of a miracle.

Love,

an about-to-be granny . . . again!

Dear Mama (I guess I'll be called that, too, one day soon . . . *gulp*!):

Your letter comes at a time in my life when I'm overwhelmed with my own anxieties and interpretations of what exactly parenthood means. You see, it took me a while to get here—to the point of being pregnant with my first child, I mean. And the journey was riddled with questions I still don't have answers to.

As a child, I loved playing with dolls, as you did. As a

teenager, I dreamed of marrying and having kids of my own. Then, as I got older and eventually married, at a point in my life where having children should have been foremost on my mind, the tables turned.

I worried that a child would impede my relationship with Matt, that the strong bond we had as husband and wife would dissipate as we turned our attention to the newest and tiniest member of our family—a baby. I struggle even now with this fear.

I worry (as all young wives do, I suppose) that I'll have to give something up in marriage in order to get something good through parenthood. Is it possible to love your husband as much after the math of your family has changed, even if you suddenly find yourself dividing your love into smaller pieces so there's enough to go around?

Then there was the *Why parenthood?* question. I heard people in our church say that they "got married to have kids." I was appalled. Kids were a *possible result* of marriage, but not the inevitable and sole outcome, right? As an adult, I've heard plenty of explanations for why couples have children: "To carry on the family name," "To leave something behind when I go," "To share my love with someone else." None struck me as particularly compelling.

At 6.5 billion, aren't there enough people on the planet already?

I suppose the best explanation I've heard for continuing to

populate the earth was this: "Christian parents raise Christian children who will carry on Christ's message of redemption and salvation to another generation."

I love this explanation, and I can't argue with it. But it still makes me a tad uncomfortable. Does God expect us, as husbands and wives, simply to be producers of soldiers for heaven's army? Are we to churn out children like doughnuts on the Krispy Kreme line so we can fill the globe with more mini-Christians?

And that raises another question: how many is enough? Some have argued with me that it's "audacious" for Christian parents to stop at two or three children when they claim money prevents them from having any more.

That's a bitter pill to swallow. Kids are expensive. And by the time they're eighteen, they will cost the average couple about $150,000. Are we as Christian parents wholly prevented from taking money into consideration when we're planning the sizes of our broods?

And then there's the faith question: I daily live in fear that something will happen to this child inside me. Every twinge, every ache, every cramp sends me flying to the phone for my OB-GYN, begging for reassurance. That fear is sin, I know, because ultimately it's faithlessness. At some point, I made the transition from thinking that having a child might be a good idea to realizing it's something I want more than anything in the world. Though now the answering of the prayer for that child comes with some risks.

I think when God grants a child to hopeful parents, it's like all answered requests—the receiver of that gift has to avoid loving the result of that prayer *so much* that she loses sight of Who gave it to her in the first place. It's not hers to keep, after all. She just gets to steward it for a while.

Now, just when you thought I'd covered every possible worry about impending parenthood, I've got another for you: what if I'm not a good parent? I know you said there are no perfect parents, just as there are no perfect kids, perfect spouses, perfect students, or perfect employees. We're fallible creatures, striving for Christ's perfection every day. But what if I'm just not good at it?

Take Tom Thumb's parents, for example:

There was once a poor farmer who was sitting by the hearth one evening and poking the fire, while his wife was spinning nearby. "How sad that we have no children!" he said. "It's so quiet here, and other homes are full of noise and life." "Yes," his wife responded with a sigh. "If only we had a child, just one, even if it were tiny and no bigger than my thumb, I'd be quite satisfied. We'd surely love him with all our hearts."[2]

As is often the case in fairy tales, their wish is granted, and the wife gives birth to a son no bigger than her thumb. Now, while these parents seem good and loving enough, the farmer and his son come upon some strangers in the woods who are so impressed with the little boy that they offer to buy him for a handsome sum. Despite his initial hesitation, and at the urging of his son (who says, "Don't you worry. Just give me away. I'll manage to get back soon"), the farmer sells the boy.[3]

Tom, it turns out, ends up in a mouse hole, a cow's stomach, and a wolf's belly before miraculously (and by his own cleverness) ending up safe at home.

I don't think the farmer and his wife were winning any parenting awards that year.

So, what happens if you make a mistake you can't take back? Fairy tales smooth even the roughest of parental mishaps, but in the real world, words and deeds have an impact on children that might not be seen for many years.

How can I live my life as a mother without being totally paralyzed by the fear of blowing it?

Love,

Sarah

Dearest Mama-to-Be:

I so appreciate the openness and honesty of your questions,

because, truth be told, there isn't a parent-to-be who hasn't asked the same questions somewhere along the way. But I want to point out that your math is wrong!

You don't have to *divide* your love up into little pieces. Your love is *multiplied* with each addition to your family. It isn't a matter of choosing to love either your husband or your baby. You love both, more deeply, more passionately than you ever thought possible. And let me tell you—you have *no* idea how much you will fall in love with your baby.

A man and a woman marry and pledge to love each other until death do them part, and out of the wellspring of their devotion comes this little one who has his father's eyes and his mother's dimples. This lamb, so fresh from heaven, will gaze at you with eyes of pure love. What he searches for in your face is the same look of adoration shining back at him.

One of my favorite guests on the radio show is Dr. Brenda Hunter. She is a brilliant psychologist and author who has an uncanny knowledge about the bond between mama and baby. She has told my listeners on multiple occasions that babies come into this world "wired to be loved by their mamas." Your baby won't care if you're not perfect. Your child wants to know you love him, and that you will always be there for him.

Parenting is really a minirepresentation of how we ourselves are designed. God made us to love Him and to be

loved by Him. Isn't that awesome? He knows we are not perfect (far from it), and yet He loves us—unconditionally, steadfastly, and eternally. Like little children, we gaze up at Him
and long to see His love manifest in our lives.

Speaking of math, you ask the question: how many children? All I can tell you is that we serve a living God who cares
about families. He designed them, so asking Him to give you
guidance as to how many or how few is a question He will
readily answer. Daddy and I prayed long and hard about the
size of our family. After God blessed us with two girls, followed by two boys, we both felt our family was complete.
We prayed before each child was conceived, all during each
pregnancy, and between pregnancies. We prayed when we
thought we were through with pregnancies. God, my dear, is
in the business of answering prayers. He will give you the
wisdom, the desire, and the peace to know what the size of
your family should and will be. Trust Him and leave your
concerns with Him!

Let me address the fear factor. There has never been a
pregnant woman who didn't have fears. It comes with the
territory, along with stretch marks and frequent trips to the
bathroom. The question is not if you will have fears, but
rather what will you do with those fears. May I suggest a
word here? Surrender. If you say you love God, and I know
you do, then you must (as we all must) learn to *trust* God. Before our Father blew the first star into heaven, He had al-

ready determined *whether* you would have children, *when* you would have children, and *what* those children would be (boys or girls). Here's where we get into the "Our God is an awesome God" part.

He is God and we are not. Pregnancy is like jumping out of an airplane without a parachute. Ultimately, only God can uphold you, and only God will catch you. Enjoy the ride!

"Sleeping Beauty" is a tale that begins with parents who wanted to have a child. They were not your ordinary parents, mind you. They were royalty:

> Once upon a time there lived a king and queen who longed for a child more than anything. Yet no child came. Then one day as the queen was bathing, a frog hopped out of the water and said to her, "Oh, Queen, before the year has ended, you will give birth to a daughter."[4]

Most of us don't have a frog to break the news. We use an early pregnancy test. But the positive results always bring an overwhelming sense of the magnificent. You know you have just stepped into something so much bigger than yourself.

In Beauty's case, her father threw a huge feast and invited a bunch of fairies. But he forgot to invite one, who in turn put a curse on the child. The curse involved a spindle and the pricking of the daughter's finger. What did Dad do? What any father would: he destroyed all the spindles in the land, except one. Still, Beauty found it, pricked her finger, and fell asleep for a hundred years.

Darling, do you see how this king went out of his way to protect his daughter? But he still blew it. He missed just one spindle. (You *do* remember that a handsome prince wakes her with a kiss, however, and the rest is fairy tale history.) No matter how much this father, who was crazy about his kid, tried to protect his little girl, she still got hurt.

There's a lesson here for parents: we must constantly surrender the care and safekeeping of our children to the King who never misses anything. He sets His angels to keep watch over our little ones. He has plans for their welfare and not their destruction. He is their Provider and Protector—the perfect Parent.

I will also let you in on a little secret. This surrendering business doesn't end when your daughter grows up, gets married, and starts a family. We parents are in the business of praying for protection for our children no matter how old they are. God has placed children in our lives for us to love and nurture. But we must never forget they are always and ultimately His. He loves your child more than you ever could.

Surrender. You *will* make mistakes, but He forgives and repairs. You *will* have fears, but His perfect love casts it all away.

You *will* feel overwhelmed, but He has made you an over comer.

Welcome to motherhood. Your life will never be the same.

Love,

your mama

9

Singleness

Mom:

I have a friend named Jen at work. She's thirty-five, beautiful, funny, sharp, and athletic. She's also single, and for the life of her, she cannot find a mate—a source of constant unhappiness and (quite vocal) complaint. So I wonder how that affects the way she relates to God. Let me explain.

I think it's a strange thing to be a woman. I say this because aside from the many eccentricities and complexities that make us unique (let it never be said a woman is a simple thing!), it struck me like a ton of bricks today thinking about Jen that we as women define ourselves most often by our relationships. Even for those of us with steely-eyed career aspirations, a life full of rewarding ministry work, or numerous personal pursuits, we tend to identify ourselves by first pointing to those we love, belong to, and associate with. Think of how we often introduce ourselves to others: "I'm Jack's wife," "I'm Annie's mother," "I'm Tim's girlfriend," "I'm Susan's friend," "I'm Mary's grandmother."

Literature recognizes the relational aspect of being a woman. After all, think of the countless fairy tales that begin with something like "There once lived a man and his wife," or "Once upon a time, there were three sisters," or "In a land far away, there lived an evil stepmother." Not gardeners, seamstresses, or musicians, but wives, mothers, sisters.

In fact, I can't think of a single fairy tale where the heroine's story ends this way: "She lived alone and contented until the end of her days." Why, it's the attainment of a spouse that often sets up that favorite ubiquitous conclusion: "And they lived happily ever after." If it's not the damsel in distress waiting for her particularly fetching captain of the rescue squad, then it's a king and queen eager to settle into retirement and desperate to find their daughter a mate because she's "of an age."

I can't help but feel these relationship banners strip from us women a bit of our individuality—after all, we classify ourselves as women by using the presence of every other person in our lives *except* our own. Does that indicate some insecurity in us, or is it an admirable death to self?

Why do we define ourselves like this?

And if we choose this path to identification, what happens to the woman who suddenly doesn't have the relationship she's used to define herself? What about the single mom? The divorcée? The widow? Who do they become?

Marriage is a relationship that's perhaps the strongest of

definers. Married woman are horses from a different herd than their single counterparts. They travel in packs, associate and re-create together, and speak a totally different language—one replete with terms like "joint checking," "double vanity," and "couples Bible study."

Singleness: now there's a topic that's always intrigued me. As you know, I married relatively late, and for a time, I wondered if God was going to let my desire for marriage go unfulfilled. I wondered what in the world I would do with my life as a single woman. The thought was mind-boggling.

As distinctly as I remember being single, I remember just as distinctly being made to feel a bit guilty because I usually had a date Friday nights. A date, mind you, not a husband. I was promised fulfillment in marriage, a lifetime of security, and the attainment of all life's desires (no offense to my husband, but I've since learned marriage ain't always Shangri-la). When, my friends asked, was I going to settle down?

Is marriage the new "in crowd"?

In 1 Corinthians 7:1, Paul remarked, "Now for the matters you wrote about: It is good for a man not to marry." He then went on to note: "Now to the unmarried and the widows I say: It is good for them to stay unmarried, as I am. But if they cannot control themselves, they should marry, for it is better to marry than to burn with passion" (vv. 8–9).

At first glance, it sounds like Paul wasn't too keen on marriage. Now, before you go moaning that all that good Christian education was wasted if I can't recognize his point here, I *do* know that Paul wasn't expressing some preference for singleness over marriage, and that Orthodox Jewish belief of the day made marriage an obligation. Paul was basically instructing that singleness was perfectly acceptable as an alternative to marriage. Single people were not second-class family members to God, and their choice to remain single was nothing to disparage.

So we know there's nothing *wrong* with being single; I don't think anyone would argue that. Here's the real conundrum: single is good, but exactly *how* good? Is it better (more sanctified) than the good that comes with marriage?

The single woman of today has more to occupy her, certainly: more career options, hobbies, travel, ministry—plenty to keep her busy. But it doesn't necessarily mean she will have an easier time defining herself in a world that classifies by relationships, or that her purpose in God's design will be any clearer.

I guess I know the answer, because God doesn't distinguish between married, single, widowed, or divorced, any more than he does yellow, black, or white.

So maybe the real question is: where does my friend Jen fit in at the church? Particularly when most believers define themselves by using the one thing (marriage) that she doesn't have?

Love,

your perplexed (and only recently unsingle) daughter

Dear Sadie, Sadie, married lady:
I remember being young and so madly in love with your dad—longing for him to ask me to marry him. During those months time crawled, and I could not, for the life of me, figure out what was taking him so long to pop the question.

But I remember doing something with that time between pining for your father and when he finally got down on bended knee to ask *the* question. What I did was a whole lot of personal inventory about who I was as a person.

If your daddy—or any other man for that matter—had not asked me to marry him, would that have made me not me? Would I be somehow less of a woman if I never married? Truth be told, don't all women ask themselves that same question somewhere along the journey of life? I really had to wrestle with the idea that marriage was not the ultimate designation of who I was. But even more important, I had to come to grips with the concept that either God was in charge of my life, or I was. We couldn't both rule my heart.

God designed us for intimacy, and for so many women, the earthly experience of that sense of oneness is marriage. But for others, it's not. Did Paul have more value in God's eyes because he was unmarried, whereas Peter was married? Didn't God love and use them both?

No one could doubt God's love for Paul. Not all of us have the kind of illuminating experience he did traveling on life's highway. But Paul's Damascus road encounter not only gave this Jew among Jews a new heart but a new vision as to where he fit into God's plan. For Paul, it was a complete and utter sellout for God. He didn't have the time or the desire to marry. He was completely committed to serving His Father, with every ounce of his being. There would have been nothing left over for a wife.

Peter, on the other hand, was married. He, like Paul, would end up losing his life because he chose to follow Christ. We know God loved Peter, even when he denied his Savior three times. And think of the breakfast they had along the shores of the Galilee when the resurrected Messiah gave Peter his assignment for life by telling him to "shepherd My sheep" and "tend My lambs" (John 21:15, 17 NASB). It doesn't get any better than having breakfast with Jesus and hearing right from His lips what He wants you to do with the rest of your life.

You and I both know single women who have sold out to Jesus as well. They have a fire in their spirits that is contagious. And like Paul, they are not married. Does that mean in the dark quiet of night they haven't wondered what marriage would be like? Have they had to deny themselves at some very deep level? Have they soaked their pillows with tears, begging God to provide mates? Maybe. We will never know. Only God hears those heart groans—and He always answers. Sometimes His answer is no. That's the tough part.

And sometimes God takes away a soul mate and a woman is left alone. She now sets the table for one, where for twenty, thirty, or maybe only two or three years, she had always set two places for dinner. After the two have been reduced to one, how does the one continue all alone? If we are going to be absolutely open and truthful with one another, the answer is she doesn't do it very easily. But she *can* do it by trusting in the One who will never leave her or forsake her. The unconditional Lover of her soul is always there—for the widow, the single woman, and for us married ladies as well.

It really is one of those basics we need to get right if we want to live right. It is all about God: who He is and who we are in Him. It cannot be about our circumstances: our marital status, our finances, our jobs, or our children. We exist *for* God *because* of God and live *through* God.

Hans Christian Andersen's "The Little Mermaid" bears no resemblance to the Disney version. This is the story of a sea creature who wanted something so desperately she was willing to make a deal with the devil. In the story, the devil is the Sea Witch, but it is a barter of the most evil kind nonetheless.

The Little Mermaid was willing to have her tongue cut out (a great loss, because she had the most beautiful voice in the sea) and drink a potion that changed her tail into legs. But the Sea Witch told her each step she took would be "like treading on a knife." She was also told that if the prince she longed for fell in love with another woman, she would lose her life: "The day after he marries someone else, you will die from a broken heart and turn to foam on the sea."[1]

It didn't matter. The Little Mermaid was so determined to marry her earthly prince that she drank the potion, got her tongue cut out, walked in excruciating pain, and you guessed it, lost at love. The prince married another, and the Princess of the Sea turned into sea foam.

Not exactly your stereotypical love story.

Andersen's point is that not everyone lives happily ever after. Our poor choices have poor consequences. Was marrying so important to the Little Mermaid that she was willing to leave all she was designed for, the family who loved her, and the world where she belonged? She was blinded by love, and it cost her life.

There is a message—or a question—in this sad story: is it better to love or to be loved? Even as a single woman, you can love: family, friends—even people from other cultures that you can serve through missions. A widow has so much to share with other women; she may be able to spare a young, impetuous wife some of the heartache and hurt caused by foolish actions.

But remember: God loves the single woman, the widow, and the married woman—eternally, divinely, absolutely, unfailingly. We are never women without love, if we are looking in the right place.

Here's our hope as women of the Word, trying to engage the world. Long before any man says to us, "I do," Jesus said, "I did." In Him, we are never women who are alone.

Love,

Mom

Mom:

I admire many of the single women I know.

I admire them because they don't run around looking for a boyfriend . . . like I did.

Once.

When I was young and foolish.

And didn't know any better.

Really, I admire them because these women have that certain strength of character that comes from knowing who they are in Christ, that certain serenity that comes with making peace with God's plans for their lives. Now, that doesn't mean they never have quiet moments of struggle with the Lord or that their single paths have been rosy. But it means they've accepted where God has them today.

I think specifically of our friend Kelly, who's a missionary in Asia—how she so calmly approaches each new day knowing she's exactly where God wants her, geographically and relationally. These single women, they *know* they are destined for singleness. So I wonder, how did they get to that point? How did Kelly know that God designed her for singleness, particularly if there was a stage in her life (which there was) where she longed for a marital relationship?

The story of the Little Mermaid breaks my heart, because the prevailing emotion that I'm left with after reading that fable is desperation. This creature gave up her family, her tail, her voice, and her home for a man she loved—someone she probably knew, from the start, wasn't the best choice for her. I mean, aside from the geography barrier, there was the fact that these two were different species. The Little Mermaid's complete willingness to assume the dangers and difficulties of her choices paints a picture of someone willing to do anything to get love.

I know countless women who have sensed that desperation in their own lives. But *desperation* is really just another word for *unhappiness*, isn't it? So what do you do when you're getting older and the desire for marriage isn't getting any weaker? What if, despite the assurances of friends and acquaintances that "Your time will come," you're worried it never will?

I guess that problem poses two questions: (1) how do you

know you're designed for marriage at all, and (2) how do you exercise patience in the interim?

As far as knowing you're designed for marriage, much as I knew Matt was "the one," I have to believe single women just *know* they are designed for singleness. This is probably a more common occurrence with men than women (we women are relational creatures, after all!), but when the desire for a husband and family fades, it may be God's way of stamping out a spark that was never to burst into flames. I've prayed God would take away certain desires in my own life, if it wasn't His will for me to have them. God's got a funny way of giving us what we ask for sometimes, and other times removing the desire for what we want in the first place.

Now, assuming a woman's desire for marriage keeps on truckin' and every rendition of Etta James's "At Last" makes her burst into sobs and she starts sending herself roses on Valentine's Day—well, then the really difficult part rolls around: being patient enough to wait for the man God wants her to have.

The Little Mermaid could be a modern-day tale about patience. The mermaid's desperation, her impetuousness, brought her face-to-face with her own destruction.

Now, don't get me wrong: I'm not pooh-poohing romantic love or the intensity of emotion felt by star-crossed lovers. You know full well that I'm Queen of the Saps.

But really, how many of us, impatient for God to make

His paths for our lives clear, rush headlong into second-best situations because we're unwilling to wait for God any longer? I've done that in my own life countless times, and I shudder to think what that could have meant for a marriage relationship. I think of a college boyfriend I *almost* married— but then ended up waiting six more years for the man of my dreams. What would have happened if I had taken the plunge earlier?

For all single women, whether confirmed bachelorettes, would-be wives, or widows, I think about what Paul wrote in Philippians 4:12: "I know what it is to be in need, and I know what it is to have plenty. I have learned the secret of being content in any and every situation, whether well fed or hungry, whether living in plenty or in want."

That's ultimately what it's all about: contentment.

I think contentment in God's language means making peace with being who—and where—He wants us to be. After all, He knows what we need, be it wisdom, a spouse, or a special ministry reserved for our singleness.

God apparently knew that I needed a husband who loved football.

And video games.

. . . Did I say something about pining for a husband?

Love,

Sarah

Part 4

Sex

Beware the Sirens, and Pipers with Rats

"Stories tell us of what we already knew and
forgot, and remind us of what we haven't yet
imagined."
—ANNE L. WATSON

10

✦

Sex and Purity

Dearest one:

I would like to talk with you about the *S*-word. Frankly, we don't discuss the *S*-word very well in the church. We stutter and stammer and trip over our words when one of our children asks, "Where do babies come from?"

Our reaction tends to be either "Ask your mother," "The other kids will tell you," or "Won't they discuss that in Sunday school?" Or worse yet, we say nothing and let MTV do the teaching, and what a lesson *that* is.

We parents cannot afford to be silent on this subject. With more than three million new cases of sexually transmitted diseases being diagnosed each year, parents literally can give their children information that could save their lives.[1]

It's funny, but providing our kids with the right facts on sexuality (there, I said the *S*-word and the kitchen floor didn't swallow me up!) has lifesaving consequences. The world can't wait to push us toward sexual activity. Sex is used to advertise everything from football games to car sales. It comes

fast and cheap through the world of entertainment. And
now, with the advent of the Internet, men (and women)
don't have to visit the seedy adult bookstores anymore. They
can download pornographic sewage right in the privacy of
their family rooms.

As a result, in this sex-saturated culture we see a higher
number of brides and grooms walking down the aisle on
their wedding days *not* being virgins. This is true both inside
and outside of the church. The statistics proving this are beyond dispute.

Where did we parents go wrong? I lived through the sixties. That was supposed to be the sexual revolution. Phrases
such as "Let it all hang out" and "If it feels good, do it" were
the watchwords of the day. But never in a million years did
we in the sixties think we would ever see what is so rampant
in the twenty-first century! Pornography is all over TV and
the movies. The top pop songs of the day blatantly sing
about it. On our computers, we get spammed during the
workday with a kind of vulgarity that defies description.

What irony that in the middle of this cultural hurricane, I,
as your mother, am supposed to instruct you on the virtues
of purity and hope that you listen to the calm winds of reason and truth. I am to tell you that sex before marriage is
wrong; it opposes God's Word, and it is hazardous to your
health. I must also tell you that once married, you must remain monogamous. Adultery is a sin, and it wreaks havoc on

a marriage. From David and Bathsheba to Bill Clinton and Monica Lewinsky, sex outside of marriage is wrong.

There, I said it. As have millions of other mothers. So why hasn't it prevented nearly thirty-five hundred abortions every day and divorces that outpace marriages?[2]

Are we just to presume this is a different day? That no one is a virgin anymore? That the old-fashioned ideas of purity and chastity have outlived their usefulness? I simply refuse to accept that.

As I look at my granddaughter, the idea of her losing her virginity before her wedding day is absolute anathema to me. She is so sweet and pure (well, as you know, your little niece is a wild two-year-old, but that is to be expected), and I think, *Surely she will remember what the Word says about fleeing youthful lusts. Clearly, she will understand that wearing white on her wedding day is a symbol of her chastity and not just a fashion statement.* But just as I think that, I start having my doubts. Can we as twenty-first-century women really live our lives with sexual purity?

Aesop, in one of his famous fables, told the story of the "One-Eyed Doe."

A doe had had the misfortune to lose one of her eyes, and could not see anyone approaching her on that side. So to avoid any danger she always used to feed on a high cliff near the sea, with her good eye looking towards the land. By this means, she could see when the hunters approached her on land, and often escaped by this means. But the hunters found out that she was blind in one eye and, hiring a boat, rowed under the cliff where she used to feed and shot her from the sea. "Ah," she cried with her dying voice, "I thought of the dangers of the land, but not those of the sea. That was my undoing."[3]

I fear too many young women today don't know their blind spot. They talk loosely about sex, dress in a provocative way, and act flippant about relationships. They don't think they can get hurt, but they do. Bad ideas and selfish desires, like the hunters in Aesop's tale, hide under the cliffs of life, waiting to attack us where we are vulnerable.

So how do we, as older women, make purity attractive? What are women your age saying about abstinence and the concept of saving their virginity until marriage? Has the idea of purity gone the way of the dodo bird? If truth is absolute and doesn't change over time, then saving oneself for marriage should be as worthy an idea now as it was in Sarah and Abraham's day.

Is "Snow White" just the name of a fairy tale or is it the condition of our hearts, once they have been cleansed from sin? Are there sins we can avoid that will make us the real princesses in the fairy tale of life?

My mama told me about sex and how precious a component it was within the bonds of marriage. I still believe that today. But I am afraid I might be part of a dying breed. What do you think?

Love,

your ancient but caring mother

Dear Mom:

Don't take this the wrong way, but I'm not necessarily *dying* to discuss sex with you. Sure, you've been accommodating and open when it comes to discussing all the uncomfortable stuff in the lives of your kids, but for some reason that topic is the great frontier none of us Parshall offspring likes to traverse. I mean, you're Mom, and it's s-e-x. Those two words might never have been intended to coexist in the same sentence.

That being said, you asked me where the parents of your generation went wrong. I don't think you did. Not entirely, anyway. Sure, there are probably parents in Christendom who could have done a better job of preparing their children for the trials of adolescence in a sex-saturated world, who could have taken more of a lead in educating their children on sex and its consequences, who could have done a better job of promoting the kind of obedience that God commands.

Yet you yourself acknowledge sex is fast and cheap in this modern world. There's only so much protecting of your kids you can do, right? (I seem to remember you writing recently both that "we must constantly surrender the care and safe-keeping of our children to the King, who never misses any-thing" and "There's no such thing as perfect parents." Even *you* recognize your influence as a parent only goes so far.)

Kids of all ages have free will. The exercise of that free will gets a little trickier when popular culture is offering up sex by the bushel. Honestly, I think we Generation Xers and Gener-ation Yers have it harder than you ever did—even back in the free-lovin' sixties. I am hard-pressed to think of anything that's truly off-limits by the world's standards.

Didn't we impeach and yet ultimately forgive the highest elected official in the land for actions related to his perjury and adultery? I mean, if the commander in chief can get away with it, isn't that a message to a million American kids that they've all got the green light?

So, purity becomes an even harder stance, an even deeper line in the sand when the rest of the world migrates in the opposite direction and calls it normal.

Purity isn't an ancient relic. It's just getting harder to exer-cise.

And don't think you, as the older generation, have to make purity more attractive for us, either. That's a responsi-bility we ought to take upon ourselves. You can instruct, admonish, and counsel, sure. But with all due respect, women look to other women their own age to determine what is not only appropriate, but attractive. We don't need anyone else preaching at us.

If anything, we need more women of my generation to be vocal about their stance on sexual purity and be visibly set apart from the rest of the world in how they carry themselves as women. After all, I will follow someone's lead if I like where she's going and what she's doing to get there.

I'm not talking about pantaloons at the pool, faces without traces of makeup, or watching only G-rated movies. Please. I'm *slightly* more cutting-edge than that.

The women of my generation simply need the tools to stand apart. This is the only way we modern women are going to catch a break as far as the battle for purity goes. Right now, I feel as if our whole generation is caught in quicksand, and the harder we try to get out, the faster we sink. So much rests not only on the ability and desire to do something, but the proper devices used to accomplish it.

Someone's got to throw us a rope.

I'm reminded of a little-known story:

There was once a stepmother who, besides her stepdaughter, had a daughter of her own. Whatever her own daughter might do, she looked kindly at her and said, "Sensible darling!" but as for the stepdaughter, whatever she might do to please, it was always taken amiss . . . and the stepmother took it in her head to drive the step-daughter from the house.[4]

At the request of her stepmother, this poor girl's father took her into a cold wood, without so much as a blanket to keep her warm, and left her to die. But as luck would have it, she wasn't there long before Morozko (known to us non-Russians as Jack Frost) happened upon her and took pity on her. "He had compassion on the girl; he wrapped her in furs, warmed her with warm coverings, and brought her a coffer, high and heavy, full of bridal garments, and gave her a robe all garnished with gold and silver."[5]

Not only did Morozko warm her and make her beautiful through the adornments he offered, but he exposed the evil deeds of her stepmother to boot. I can't imagine the girl would have lived long in the wood without the right clothing. Not only did he save her from ruin, but as someone wiser than herself, he literally transformed her life from one of rags to one of riches.

She would have been stuck in a hopeless situation without the assistance of Jack Frost, who gave her the tools for turning her circumstances around.

So, what are the tools for sexual purity? Here's my list: instruction, illustration, and dedication. My generation's women need older women who are going to instruct on purity, peers who will illustrate the proper examples and behaviors of purity, and their own resolute commitment to exercising that purity no matter what the culture says.

Again, as for your question about where you—parents of the baby-boom generation—went wrong, you didn't. You just need to make sure your generation keeps telling us what you've told us in the past. Give us the lessons and teach us the principles. The rest is up to us.

Purity is hard to maintain. After all, we've read: "Who can say, 'I have kept my heart pure; / I am clean and without sin'?" (Prov. 20:9). Purity is really relative, because we're always messing up, all the time. How many of us are really "pure"?

Well, I guess the answer is this: purity starts with being pure at heart. The pure see things from a pure perspective. The corrupted, on the other hand, see *nothing* as pure (Titus 1:15). The tools for practicing sexual purity sure aren't going to come from popular culture. How could they? That's like asking a dung beetle what it feels like to be a swan.

Now, we swans, we've got to stick together.

It's the only way we're going to stand firm and stand out in a dung-beetle world.

Love,

Sarah

-☼-

Dearest Sarah:

Thank you for the words of encouragement, for saying that maybe I didn't do so badly when it comes to that old *S*-word. But thank you even more for reminding me that the challenge to be pure is really *ever* before us, married or single.

Do you remember Jesus talked about purity when He spoke to a crowd on a mountainside somewhere in Galilee? We call this discourse the Beatitudes—a word derived from the Latin noun *beatitudo*, which means "blessed." Among the items Jesus listed in His invitation to grow deeper in discipleship was the concept of purity. He said:

"Blessed are the pure in heart, / for they will see God" (Matt. 5:8).

What an intriguing and mysterious statement! What *did* Jesus mean when He called us to heart purity? Remember when you and I went to Israel and walked around the temple ruins in Jerusalem? We learned the high priests of the temple practiced many ritualistic types of washing, thinking that if they purified themselves on the outside, they might, at the same time, become sinless on the inside.

They were wrong, and that is why Jesus made a point of talking about the states of our hearts rather than the cleanliness of our hands. The most important purity is the kind that stems from the heart. We become pure from the inside out, not the other way around. When we make God the most important part of our lives, He affects every part of our lives.

The right choices regarding sexual behavior become crystal clear when He is first in our hearts.

But there is another mysterious part to Jesus' statement: "They shall see God." No one has seen the face of God yet. But the very last book of the Bible says someday that will change: "They will see His face, and His name will be on their foreheads" (Rev. 22:4).

Awesome! We will really behold Him face-to-face. Have you thought what that will be like? We will look the King of all creation, the Lord of all lords, the great I AM, right in the face. I am light-headed at the very thought of being in His presence. And you know what? He will know us and call us by name. That same book of the Bible says not only will He wipe away every tear, but He also promises us a brand-new name (2:17). I wonder what mine will be. I like my name, but being named by God is an amazing thought!

I know He will look on my face, and I on His. But even more important, He will look at my heart. What will He see: my selfishness, my disappointment, my anger, my fears, my sorrows? I don't have to wait until that glorious day, for I know He looks at my heart today. First Samuel 16:7 tells us that we look at the outsides of one another, but God looks on the inside. He sees all the rotten, sinful stuff we try so hard to hide from one another. But He also sees the woman who loves God and wants to live for Him. He sees beyond the failures and finds the child longing to be loved by her heavenly Daddy. With Christ in our hearts, He sees the purity we ourselves could never bring about. We have been scrubbed clean by the power of the Cross.

You challenge me, daughter, to be a Titus woman in your life. My job is to instruct you to "be self-controlled and pure" (Titus 2:5). That is, at the same time, both humbling and daunting, because I so passionately desire to model biblical womanhood for you.

In one of his famous fables, Aesop talked about the power of imitating good behavior.

> One fine day two Crabs came out from their home to take a stroll on the sand. "Child," said the mother, "you are walking very ungracefully. You should accustom yourself to walking straight forward without twisting from side to side."
>
> Pray, Mother," said the young one, "do but set the example yourself, and I will follow you."[6]

Like the mother crab, I want to teach you to walk gracefully by walking in His love; to prevent you from twisting back and forth with the world's inane ideas of sexual expression. I teach you best by living as an example, so I myself must learn not to twist from side to side but rather walk uprightly before the Lord.

My darling daughter, if you desire to have a heart after His, then the purity you seek will emanate from the inside out. You won't need standards, or models or ropes or tools. You just have to have a heart that pants after Him. It's a heart He sees; it's a heart He loves. And someday, you will see the face of the One who has always loved your pure heart. What a day that will be!

I'll close now, because I have some sand-walking to do.

Love,

your mama

11
·ᢡ·
Homosexuality

Mom:

I have friends who are gay. These friendships started early—in high school, I think, when I determined I wasn't going to relegate myself to one crowd but befriend everyone, even those who were unpopular, outsiders, different. This kind of philosophy attracted all sorts of people, including some homosexuals, who were always different from the rest of the students. They were some of my closest friends.

As an adult, though, I find myself struggling more with the concept of homosexuality. Age and maturity have a way of forcing you to come to grips with what it means for someone to be gay, and exactly what the Bible says about it.

Taking God's Word as absolute truth (which we as Christians have no choice but to do) and knowing God spoke through mankind to author this book (rather than thinking the Bible was the product of men caught up in their own spiritual or political agendas) makes it pretty clear homosexuality is unacceptable in God's eyes:

God gave them over to shameful lusts. Even their women ex-changed natural relations for unnatural ones. In the same way the men also abandoned natural relations with women and were inflamed with lust for one another. Men committed indecent acts with other men, and received in themselves the due penalty for their perversion. (ROM. 1:26–27)

So, clearly homosexuality is a sin, but what I read in 1 Corinthians worries me: "Do you not know that the wicked will not inherit the kingdom of God? Do not be deceived: Neither the sexually immoral nor idolaters nor adulterers nor male prostitutes nor homosexual offenders . . . will inherit the kingdom of God" (6:9–10).

This verse says explicitly that homosexual offenders will not partake in the kingdom of God. But isn't homosexuality, after all, a sin just like every other sin? What is to prevent someone from asking for forgiveness of that sin, inviting Jesus to sit on the throne of his or her heart, and still spend eternity with the Lord? Liars, adulterers, tax evaders, and murderers can, if they accept Christ, enter the kingdom, so why not gays?

I had a friend in college—a pastor's kid—who called himself an "evangelical homosexual." He knew Scripture better than I did, faithfully attended church, led Bible studies, and lived in almost all ways as a Christian would be expected to live. He made it seem possible to be both a Christian and a homosexual. So I ask you: is it?

Everyone approaches the homosexual differently. Some ostracize, some ridicule, others picket, protest, and lobby (I've seen the hateful signs at some rallies that make me cringe for the church as a whole—God *doesn't hate* the homosexual, just the sin that separates him or her from the Lord). Homosexuals repulse many Christians, in much the same way one slimy toad repulsed a lovely princess once: "In olden times, when wishing still helped, there lived a king whose daughters were all beautiful, but the youngest was so beautiful that the sun itself, which had seen so many things, was always filled with amazement each time it cast rays upon her face."[1]

As the familiar story goes, this lovely girl had lost her golden ball in a deep well, and the only one capable of retrieving it was a frog with a thick, ugly head. In return for his kindness, the princess promised, at the frog's request, that she would love him and let him be her companion and playmate. All he wanted was a friend.

Well, the princess promptly dropped the nice-girl act once the ball was back in her possession.

The poor frog insisted on making the princess keep her promise. He hopped all day to get to the castle, and when the princess tried to refuse his entry, the king, her wise father, said: " 'If you've made a promise, you must keep it. Go and let him in.' After she went and opened the door, the frog hopped in the room . . . where he plopped himself down and cried out, 'Lift me up beside you!' She refused, until the king finally ordered her to do so."[2]

The princess continued to act like a brat until her father finally scolded, "It's not proper to scorn someone who helped you when you were in trouble!"[3]

From the start of this story, my heart breaks for the little frog. How cruel to have someone turn her back on you for no other reason than that you are different. I feel the same way about my gay friends who are shunned. How many of us have turned our backs on these people because the sin was so abhorrent to us that we forgot the sinner? Does the great King have to remind us, like the princess, that we are to keep our promise to "love one another" (John 13:35)?

I struggle with an opposite tendency: loving my gay friends too much. What I mean by that is they are such close companions of mine that I willingly overlook the sin to maintain the friendship. After all, who am I—a sinner saved by grace, with more sins than I care to acknowledge—to point out somebody else's immorality?

I don't know what behavior the Lord requires of me here. And I never want to be known as judgmental.

We Christians have plenty of that to go around.

Love,

Sarah

Daughter:

There is no greater challenge to the church today than to speak the "truth in love." And nowhere is that challenge put more squarely in front of us than in the area of homosexuality.

Gay activists have plenty of political clout. They have permeated television and film, where we now see more homosexual characters than ever before. Some churches actually put into leadership those who openly engage in this sexual sin. And now, the fait accompli is an attempt to radically redefine marriage as something other than what God Himself defined.

But by the same token, in the midst of the lobbying, the media propaganda, and the drive for public policy that supports the gay lifestyle, there live people who are caught in the snare of sin. Is it possible to *truly* love the sinners but hate the sin? It is, and we must.

We sometimes act today as if homosexuality is a new sin. It isn't. Homosexual prostitutes were part of pagan worship during Old Testament days. Paul wrote his letter to the church at Rome during a time when sexual sin was rampant in the Greco-Roman world. In fact, Roman law actually contained legislation regarding homosexual behavior and protected its citizens *against* homosexual acts. But if you were a slave or a non-Roman, you didn't receive the same protection.

This goes to the core of your question regarding the passage in 1 Corinthians 6. Paul was writing to an elite Roman world where sex outside of marriage (heterosexual *and* homosexual) was tolerated. In the Christian community then, as now, it is not. Why? Because God Himself calls that behavior "sin."

Paul listed some of those sins in the passage in 1 Corinthians—sexual immorality, idolatry, adultery, and male prostitution (*all* sexual sins)—and he also added thieves, drunkards, slanderers, swindlers, and the greedy. But the most important part of that passage says: "And that is what some of you *were*" (6:11).

Do you see? What Paul was telling us is that change is possible. We can turn from our wicked ways and receive a fresh, clean start. Paul continued by telling us, "You were washed, you were sanctified, you were justified in the name of the Lord Jesus Christ and by the Spirit of our God" (6:11). Honey, that is the best wash, spin, and rinse cycle any of us can ever have!

We, the church, need to lovingly remind people who are ensnared in sexual sin that there is a way out. In a sex-saturated culture, the roar of the world often covers the message of forgiveness and redemption. We the church must bring that message to a hurting and dying world.

But here's where it gets tough. Some, in this particular group of sinners, come to Washington and demand rights that protect their sin. It's hard *not* to react to that; the behavior can be deadly to the practitioner and is anathema to God's Word. In all my years in the nation's capital, I have yet to see a march sponsored by the National Adulterers Association. *That* sin attempts to clothe itself in secrecy and doesn't demand legislative protection. But homosexual sin wraps itself in the garment of civil rights and shouts for tolerance and inclusion.

The church must learn to draw a line of distinction between the demands for policy changes and the person who truly lives in a world of deception. Too often we come across as haters rather than lovers. It is love, not hate, that draws each of us to the Cross.

I am touched by the love you have for your gay friends. By loving them, you act like Jesus. But pray about the ways in which you can love them without endorsing what they do. Easy? No. But mandatory for the saints who want to see the intersection of their faith with the culture in which they live.

Recently, when I did a program on homosexuality, I got an e-mail from a listener from whom I hear quite regularly. I truly care for this fellow. He is well known in the homosexual community as a pioneer for so-called gay rights. Yet he listens to my program consistently. I am so glad because I truly pray he will hear something about the *real* Lover of his soul who will help him escape the darkness where he currently resides.

In his e-mail, he stated that adultery was not a sin but a breach of contract. He also said that the mode of the breach happens to be sexual, and that is quite irrelevant to the nature of adultery. Do you see how confused and distorted his thinking is? He believes that homosexual sin is *not* sin, and adultery is not sexual sin but a breach of contract.

Jesus didn't excuse sin. Neither can we. But we must be reflective of the love of Christ without condoning the sin of our friends. Love your friends, daughter, but do it without affirming the sin.

There is an old nonsense verse that says:

> There was an Old Man on a hill,
> Who seldom, if ever, stood still;
> He ran up and down
> In his grandmother's gown,
> Which adorned that Old Man on a hill.

Was this code for someone who was a transvestite? Some of the nonsense poems of earlier years were actually filled with codes for hidden statements, many of them political. We may never know the secret of this little verse, but I think it is safe to say the Old Man had some kind of gender confusion.

We, as Christians, are not to add to the cultural confusion.

We must speak plainly the truth that *all* sex outside of marriage is wrong, that we must remain faithful to our mates, as God directed, *in* marriage. And at the same time, we can tell anyone struggling with sexual sin that "such were some of [us]."

I appreciate your tender heart so very much.

Love your friends who struggle with this particular sin. Love them without condoning what they do, but live your life in such a way as to woo them to the love that truly sets them free.

I love you very much.

Mom

Dear Mom:

We're talking about a difficult task here. Loving the sinner and hating the sin is like five-hundred-level theology, though it sounds *so* easy.

"I love you, but I hate what you're doing."

Simple, right?

But what a hard distinction that "sin and sinner" thing is! Especially when it comes to homosexuality. I mean, gays and lesbians identify themselves by the very thing we recognize as sin: intimate, same-sex relationships. It's like wearing a uniform for Team Transgression. Makes them kind of hard to miss, you know?

I think Jesus had a wonderful, touching way of exposing the sin of sinners while simultaneously making them feel loved. But I have to think, *Yes, but he was Jesus. He would have known the absolutely perfect way to go about doing that.* Think for a minute about the woman he encountered in the Temple courts.

> The teachers of the law and the Pharisees brought in a woman caught in adultery. They made her stand before the group and said to Jesus, "Teacher, this woman was caught in the act of adultery. In the Law Moses commanded us to stone such women. Now what do you say?" . . . [Jesus] straightened up and said to them, "If any one of you is without sin, let him be the first to throw a stone at her." . . . Jesus . . . asked her, "Woman, where are they? Has no one condemned you?" "No one, sir," she said. "Then neither do I condemn you," Jesus declared. "Go now and leave your life of sin." (JOHN 8:3–5, 7, 10–11)

The Pharisees were doing what some Christians like to do: drag a sinner in front of a group of other Christians and condemn her "according to the law" (or the Bible). Don't you remember times in your own spiritual journey where "prayer requests" were doled out as opportunities to gossip and criticize?

Jesus defused this situation, intended to lead to the woman's death, by reminding the Pharisees that for all their bombastic arrogance, they were sinners just as she was. In fact, Jesus made a point of telling this adulteress He did not condemn her.

Jesus did, though, make one final and very important statement: "Go now and leave your life of sin."

That "sin no more" part is the harder one to practice.

You pointed out that it's possible to change. I know that, too, even though I'm not an anthropologist or geneticist. I know it just because the Bible says we are new creatures in Christ. To me, that means that if a person accepts Christ as Savior, revolutionary change is possible.

But when do I have the right (or the obligation) to tell someone else to change?

Does hating the sin mean that (aside from not sinning myself) I even have to act in a certain way to make my displeasure known? How should I express my hatred of sin exactly? Obviously I'm not supposed to walk around with a placard that says, "I hate homosexuality!" Besides, it seems to be clear we Christians shouldn't judge those outside the church (1 Cor. 5:9–13). The homosexuals in the church—the ones who profess salvation—because they are brothers and sisters in Christ, should be confronted (Matt. 18:15-17); but as far as the unsaved gay or lesbian goes (and I'm guessing this is a majority of them), I think we really have to let the Lord deal with them directly.

I also worry that some Christians like to focus the "morality beam" on one sinful lifestyle in particular. Homosexuality is always a hot-button topic. But what about cheating on your taxes? Telling "little white lies"? Cutting someone off on the freeway? If we're going to be vocal about what the Bible defines as sin, then shouldn't we be equal-opportunity stone throwers?

I don't know what the right answer is on this one, because I won't take my biblical values out of my public life any more than my gay friends will necessarily always want to take the homosexuality out of theirs.

I guess that for all of us sinners, it always comes down to the power of transformation. Like many good stories, even though change seems uncomfortable, "happily ever after" is really never possible without transformation.

Remember the Frog King in our fairy tale? The story didn't end with his pining for companionship with a repulsed hostess:

> When he fell to the ground, he was no longer a frog, but a prince with kind and beautiful eyes. So, in keeping with her father's wishes, she accepted him as her dear companion and husband, whereupon the prince told her that a wicked witch had cast a spell over him and no one could have got him out of the well except her.[4]

As it turns out, that flawed and bratty princess was the only one with the power to loose the Frog King from the clutches of evil, the only one with the capacity to help him to realize who he really was.

I suppose I'm like that princess. Reluctant, and *sometimes* bratty, sure. But more important, I have the power to introduce my gay friends to freedom. You see, they're caught in the clutches of an evil reality—the broken world that's unforgiving and heartless. If that world has transformed them into who they are, then it is only Christ's transforming power that can help them become who they have the potential to be.

I don't like having to tell other people they have the power to change—it's uncomfortable, it seems audacious, it sounds rude! But there's no point in politeness when you're trying to save someone.

God, it seems, can use even the most unwilling of instruments to set a captive free.

That's good news for the reluctant . . . like me.

Love,

your daughter

12

Addiction, Pornography, and Adultery

Darling daughter:

I am writing this letter as a cautionary note of concern. Today I did a radio program on addiction, and the response was overwhelming. Callers, identifying themselves only as "anonymous" and addicted to everything from drugs to gambling, poured forth their stories of lives out of control.

America is a hurting place right now. Look at the numbers: Children who grow up in single-parent homes are twice as likely to become addicts or substance abusers. We females are three times more likely to become addicted to something if we live with only one parent; males are four times more likely. Nearly half of those who struggle with addiction are professionals or people who hold management positions.[1] And experts that come on my show tell me that 50 percent of addicts are college graduates.[2]

Sort of breaks a lot of stereotypes, doesn't it?

One particularly dark area of concern is the rise of Internet pornography. Wait! Before you roll your eyes in disgust, you need to know what a horrific problem this is. Groups such as Promise Keepers and Focus on the Family have reported that the number one issue men in the church are dealing with right now is pornography. There was once a stigma attached to going down to the seedy part of town and hoping no one would see you slip into the "adult" bookstore. Now, with the advent of the Internet, your husband, your pastor, your father, you—anyone can easily access the most unthinkable filth. Once those images get into the eyes, they quickly work their way to the heart—and they cause a kind of heart disease that is deadly.

Robert Browning's sad tale "The Pied Piper of Hamelin" addressed the problem of a "famous Hanover City" that was plagued with rats.

> Rats!
> They fought the dogs and killed the cats,
> And bit the babies in the cradles,
> And ate the cheeses out of the vats,
> And licked the soup from the cooks' own ladles,
> Split open the kegs of salted sprats,
> Made nests inside men's Sunday hats,
> And even spoiled the women's chats,
> By drowning their speaking
> With shrieking and squeaking
> In fifty different sharps and flats.[3]

The rats were everywhere, just like pornography. It's in music, film, television, video games, magazines, books, and the Internet. Like the folks in Hamelin who didn't have to look to find the rats, you don't have to look very hard to find pornography. In fact, you actually have to *look away* to avoid it!

This is not a new problem, even with all our twenty-first-century technology. Paul wrote to the church at Corinth about the subject of sexual bondage:

> *Do you not know that your bodies are members of Christ himself? Shall I then take the members of Christ and unite them with a prostitute? Never! Do you not know that he who unites himself with a prostitute is one with her in body? For it is said, "The two will become one flesh." But he who unites himself with the Lord is one with him in spirit. Flee from sexual immorality. All other sins a man commits are outside his body, but he who sins sexually sins against his own body.* (1 COR. 6:15–18)

My friend Kay Arthur says that using pornography is the equivalent of committing adultery. She explains that since sin begins in the heart, lusting after a woman in an image, a download, or a centerfold is the equivalent of breaking the marriage bonds. I agree with her. Getting sexually aroused through pornography is cheating on your mate, no matter how you define that word.

By the way, I always bristle at the idea that using pornography is a harmless act. It violates the concept of sexual intimacy as the ultimate expression of a love between a husband and wife. But porn also denigrates women and lowers them to the level of sexual playthings whose sole purpose for existing is to satisfy the lusts of men.

With the advent of child pornography, we shouldn't be so amazed that there are countless child abductions every year. It's one thing to see a child on a Web site being used for sexual exploitation. It is quite another (but equally disturbing) to see a child's image on a milk carton or on the back of a semi. Sadly, the user of Internet porn too often feels the need to act out on some sick fantasy, and when that happens, it becomes the lead story on the evening news.

Consider again the story of the Pied Piper. If you remember the tale, the village would not "pay the piper" (yes, that's where that saying comes from) after he removed all the rats from the village, so the piper sought revenge. He placed his long pipe to his lips and played a mesmerizing tune.

> Out came the children running,
> All the little boys and girls,
> With rosy cheeks and flaxen curls,
> And sparkling eyes and teeth like pearls,
> Tripping and skipping, ran merrily after
> The wonderful music with shouting and laughter.[4]

The children followed the piper into a mountain cave. Once they were inside, the mountain shut fast, and the children were lost to the village forever. It is truly a tale of woe. But there is a modern application here.

Pornography is like the Pied Piper. It sings an alluring song of sexual satisfaction while steadfastly taking the user, the addict, into a place where he is sequestered in bondage, cut off from the ones he loves. The addict thinks the rodents of daily life can be chased away by the melody of gratification. But in truth, following the piper only leads to a kind of captivity of the heart.

Paul encouraged those who struggled in this area to remember that they were "bought at a price." Because of that purchase, we must "honor God with [our bodies]" (1 Cor. 6:20).

I am warning you, because I love you, to be very careful about what you watch on TV or see in videos. Don't ever think it is harmless, lest you start following a piper who wants to imprison your heart.

Love,

your older, and hopefully wiser, mom

✳

Dear older and wiser Mama:

Addiction sounds so evil, so extreme, doesn't it? Like a terminal illness or a three-headed monster. Something "other people" struggle with. But I was thinking today about how it's really rooted in who we are as humans. I mean, we fallen creatures love getting things, having things, cherishing things. I think about Gollum from *The Lord of the Rings*. It's in our sin nature to want more. Maybe one way to view addiction is to see it as our sin nature on steroids. It's compulsive, self-perpetuating, and for the addict, larger than life. So, the object of the addiction then becomes, as Gollum says, "My precious!"

In reading your letter, I did an inventory of my life, and while I don't *think* I have any harmful addictions (there is, of course, that unfortunate shoe-buying habit), what disturbed me was how many of those who become addicts are like me. What is it about the educated, the gainfully employed, and even the Christian, that makes them trade the gold of their blessings for the grime of addiction?

That's why your example of pornography is apt and disturbing at the same time. Pornography is the biggest business on the Internet—to the tune of more than $5 billion a year. And it's a huge problem in, among other places, the Christian church. Anyone who believes differently has scales on their eyes. A whopping 44 percent of pastors admit to having visited an online porn site.[5]

As for me, I hate pornography. I mean, it's ugly, seedy, sinister (isn't all sin kind of like that at first glance?). What hit me, though, as I read your letter was what a truly degrading enterprise it is for the female participants. Someone can try to tell me that those women willingly subject themselves to that kind of treatment, and I'll say, "*Sure*. We've all got free will, don't we?"

But it's kind of like getting a tattoo on your face: you've got the power to do it, but that doesn't make it any less stupid, any less ugly, or any less permanent.

And I'll tell you something else: all that ridiculous filth makes it hard on the rest of us normal women. Think about Pamela Anderson, Jenna Jameson, or whoever the treat of the day is, flaunting a hypersensationalized, overly plastic image of "perfect" sexuality. These women could be drawing boyfriends, brothers, sons, and husbands away from their families, their loved ones, and into a fantasy world where reality is distorted, and pleasure always looks immediate.

Instant gratification: isn't that what it's really all about?

Pornography, I think, is the *ultimate* selfish act. Now, I know there are women who struggle with it, too (our sin nature is pretty curious—we've all wondered about forbidden fruit at one point or another), but let's look specifically at men, particularly because the incidence of sexual addiction and pornography use is higher with them.

A man who views pornography doesn't want emotional

involvement. He doesn't want to have to ask the girl on the screen how her day was or take the trash out for her or discuss the budget. He just wants to have his needs met and control a situation that will, if left unchecked, eventually take him down a path not to control, but to utter chaos. He wants something in his life provided *exactly* the way he wants it—consequences be hanged—and he doesn't want to have to work for it. Essentially, all he cares about is himself.

That is, I think, what makes something like porn attractive, what makes the distasteful desirable. At bottom, it's really a craving for *something else*—a need unfulfilled, a desire stifled. That something is what feeds the curiosity, that feeds the exploration, that meets the need (we think!), that feeds the addiction. That something is the siren song for the addict. Which reminds me of a familiar tale:

> The Sirens were sea-nymphs who had the power of charming by their song all who heard them, so that the unhappy mariners were irresistibly impelled to cast themselves into the sea to their destruction. Circe directed Ulysses to fill the ears of his seamen with wax, so that they should not hear the strain; and to cause himself to be bound to the mast, and his people to be strictly enjoined, whatever he might say or do, by no means to release him till they should have passed the Sirens' island. Ulysses obeyed these directions. He filled the ears of his people with wax, and suffered them to bind him with cords firmly to the mast. As they approached the Sirens' island,

the sea was calm, and over the waters came the notes of music so ravishing and attractive that Ulysses struggled to get loose, and by cries and signs to his people begged to be released; but they, obedient to his previous orders, sprang forward and bound him still faster.[6]

In Homer's epic poem *The Odyssey*, Ulysses deliberately exposed himself to the very thing he was explicitly warned against: the Sirens. Why not fill his ears with wax like the rest of the crew? Think of how much better Ulysses would have fared on his trip had curiosity not got the better of him!

How do you kill the curiosity that ultimately leads to an addiction? I guess the key is to find the need and meet it (or perhaps I should say, take it to the One who can meet it) before the what-ifs and the what's-the-harms take hold.

It could be a desire for appreciation, a need for sexual intimacy, a longing for missing trust, a need for respect, or a faltering self-esteem that fuels the flames of addiction. In pornography, it's probably a combination of all these things. These needs strike us educated Christians, us job-holders, just as they strike unbelievers collecting unemployment. And we trade up the good we have for the bad we like, because we think we know best what will satisfy our desires.

All of us have needs: food, clothing, shelter, love, affection, respect, security. But as humans we are always failing to meet those needs consistently for another person—that's part of the dilemma of cohabiting this planet with a bunch of other sinners. And maybe that's what makes us so susceptible to addiction. We're all fallen creatures, with only one hope for a lasting solution to our needs.

Try to meet your needs any other way, and you may as well throw yourself to the Sirens.

But we Christians don't have an excuse when we fall into the snare of pornography. We're *supposed* to rely wholly on God as the One who meets all our needs; we've got the tools to resist that "irresistible" siren song. So, why can I name you several men at my church who have expressed their own struggles with pornography?

And *why* pornography at all? I don't hear talk about church members' struggles with stealing, coveting, lying, tax evasion. Does it happen? Maybe. Is it rampant? Maybe not. Pornography, on the other hand, is the silent behemoth in the body, hulking and ugly and impossible to ignore; it's a problem so big that no one knows quite how to address it.

What's the pull for a Christian—someone who in theory ought to be repulsed by that kind of sexual sin?

And speaking of sexual sins, you mentioned something Kay Arthur had said to you—that using pornography is the equivalent of committing adultery. Instead of being *equivalent* to adultery, what if pornography is actually the open door to adultery? If a man starts a lustful relationship with a woman on a computer screen, he's already hiding it from his wife, concealing it from the church body. If he's already cheating on his mate with pornography, cheating on his mate with another person becomes that much easier, doesn't it? Those men I know who struggle with pornography . . . are their marriages at risk?

I guess I'm kind of discouraged by what I see around me. Pornography disgusts me; adultery disgusts me. They're sins against our own bodies, after all (1 Cor. 6:18)! But what disgusts me more is how my brothers and sisters in Christ are falling for these sins.

I guess I don't see how a failure rate like ours is acceptable, especially for a church body that ought to know better.

Love,

your daughter

Dear young woman and precious daughter:
If sexual sin disgusts you, imagine what God thinks about it! You are right. There is a huge problem in this area in the church, and we had better take care of it before more marriages are destroyed and more churches acquire a blemished witness. How *do* we fix this problem? One marriage at a time.

That old writer of Ecclesiastes was one smart fellow. He

said there was "nothing new under the sun" (1:9), and he was right. Pornography has been around almost since time began; the Internet just makes its delivery faster! Adultery is just as old a sin, and it still plagues us today.

When I was a little girl in Sunday school, we used to sing a song that was designed to teach us about our choices in satisfying our appetites—the hungers of our hearts.

> Oh, be careful, little eyes, what you see,
> Oh, be careful, little eyes, what you see.
> For the Father up above
> Is looking down in love;
> Oh, be careful, little eyes, what you see.

There was no such thing as Internet pornography back then, but the truth of that little ditty so perfectly applies today. If we are not careful about what we look at—X-rated movies, pornographic images, sex-saturated magazines—we will arouse in us a giant that is difficult to tame. When the giant awakes, he walks, in many cases, right out of a marriage and into the arms of another man or woman.

The eye gate is a passageway to the heart. Sin and lust begin in the heart, so using pornography is a kind of adultery. You might not know the name of the image you're viewing on the Internet or in the video, but the point is not the identification of the person you're lusting after; rather it's that you *are* lusting, and that is sin.

For many users of pornography, looking isn't enough. Passions are awakened, and the desire to act on those passions becomes paramount. If the husband or wife won't respond in accordance with the images in the magazines or on the Internet, the wheels are set in motion for seeking intimacy somewhere other than in the marriage bed.

I've said that we haven't done a particularly good job of teaching about sex in the church. Oftentimes we have felt it a decidedly unspiritual topic, or worse, too carnal to talk about in a sermon. Yet we leave our churches on Sunday for a world that's sexually starving and incapable of controlling its sensual appetites.

Let's get back to the basics, darling. God designed sex. *God*. Not MTV. He placed it in Eden, making it a part of His plan for perfection. He designed it as the most profound way to communicate intimacy and oneness between a man and a woman. He brilliantly uses it as a way of showing the oneness that we the church will share someday with the Bridegroom. The King of creation marvelously orchestrated it for husbands and wives to truly enjoy one another—completely, wholly, deeply.

Then along comes the great Deceiver, who, as always, messes everything up. He takes God's perfection and turns it into perversion. He takes the beautiful and makes it base and bawdy. He lies about where this oneness should take place and gets us to buy into shallow and deceptive philosophies such as "It's all good," and "Whatever floats your boat."

Wrong, wrong, and wrong. Do I make myself clear? There are no ands, ors, ifs, or buts here. No sex outside of marriage—and no sex before marriage. Black and white, crystal clear, no ambiguity. But boy, do we mess this one up.

Why? Yes, pornography plays a big role here, but so do situational ethics. You can hear such rationalizations as "My wife wasn't meeting my needs" or "I just don't love him anymore" in the church foyer, reminding us there *is* nothing new under the sun. We abandon truth for "felt needs."

Proverbs has a whole chapter devoted to adultery. The deeper meaning of the passage is meant to address the adultery of worshiping another god besides the One true living God. But the words can also be taken at face value.

> *I have covered my bed with colored linens from Egypt.*
> *I have perfumed my bed with myrrh, aloes and cinnamon.*
> *Come, let's drink deep of love till morning;*
> *let's enjoy ourselves with love!*
> *My husband is not at home;*
> *he has gone on a long journey.*
> *He took his purse filled with money*
> *and will not be home till full moon.* (PROV. 7:16–20)

The language might not be twenty-first century, but the message certainly is. The next verse reads, "With persuasive words she led him astray; / she seduced him with her smooth talk" (v. 21). Oh, be careful, little ears, what you hear!

Tend to your marriage bed, my daughter. Love your husband in both word and deed. Listen to him, because someone else could gladly play the part of the "caring" friend and lead him down a path of destruction. Communication is important—so talk *and* listen.

One of the strange stories from the *Arabian Nights* is the tale of "Scheherazade." It begins: "The Sultan Schahriar had a wife whom he loved more than all the world, and his greatest happiness was to surround her with splendour, and to give her the finest dresses and the most beautiful jewels."[7]

The sky was the limit with goodies from her husband, yet the sultan's wife had to start messing around. How foolish can a girl get?

> It was therefore with the deepest shame and sorrow that he accidentally discovered, after several years, that she had deceived him completely, and her whole conduct turned out to have been so bad that he felt himself obliged to carry out the law of the land, and order the Grand-Vizier to put her to death.[8]

Today the story would have ended in divorce. But in his sorrow, the sultan ended up marrying a new woman every day and having her murdered at night. Not exactly a tender bedtime story. The cycle of violence stopped only when a young woman named Scheherazade married him and charmed him each night with storytelling. In other words, somebody was talking to him, someone took the time to listen—and the sultan was satisfied.

Guard your heart, my darling. Keep a close eye on what you *watch*, both you and your husband. Ask the Lord to give you a sensitive spirit so you will quickly recognize when appetites get out of control.

But most important of all, learn to love your husband as Christ has loved you: tenderly, carefully, and compassionately. If you do that, no one will ever lead him, or you, astray.

Love,

your very happily married mother

Part 5

Treasures

The Queen Was in the Counting House, Counting Out Her Money

"You and I have need of the strongest spell that
can be found to wake us from the evil
enchantment of worldliness."

—C. S. LEWIS

13

Money and Debt

Mom:

Today is Saturday, housecleaning day (and the only way I'm able to survive the football season with my sanity intact). So I put on the soundtrack to *Cabaret*, and halfway through a high kick with the Clorox, "Money Makes the World Go Round" stopped me in my tracks.

If you had told me as a teenager that one of the biggest sources of anxiety and frustration in adulthood would be money, I would never have believed it.

Why would I? We weren't raised in a family where money was a major topic of discussion or concern. Sure, as an adult I can appreciate how feeding six on a single salary was probably a struggle, but all we kids were aware of was that there was enough to eat and wear. I don't think I ever had a conscious thought about money until I was in college. Idyllic? No doubt.

And it's probably the same reason I'd have told you that you were crazy if you had said, "You know, you and your husband *may possibly, occasionally*, fight about money at some point in your marriage."

Fight about money? Never, I might have replied. We were going to live happily ever after. And we were not going to worry about paying the mortgage on the castle, either.

Yet now I am a thirty-year-old woman, in a household with two incomes and no children of my own yet, and there are times when Matt and I fight because we find it difficult to make ends meet. Not because there isn't enough money, but because there's too much debt. Cars, mortgage, student loans—it adds up faster than the breakfast buffet line at Bob Evans's on a Saturday.

I'm loathe to admit it, but I've often been angry at God precisely because He let me bring this heaping pile of financial obligation on my own head (kind of ironic, isn't it, considering it was my signature on the student loan form, not God's?). I mean, what conceivable purpose is there in debt? I know the earthly answer, of course. It's to allow us to acquire something we want or need immediately even though we don't have the cash. But why does God *allow* us to get into debt at all?

Here's where I'm really confused: it seems to me the Bible itself explicitly spurns indebtedness (or at least commands that you better repay what you owe as quickly as possible). Think about this verse: "Do not be a man who strikes hands in pledge / or puts up security for debts" (Prov. 22:26).

And how about this one:

> Give everyone what you owe him: *If you owe taxes, pay*
> *taxes; if revenue, then revenue; if respect, then respect; if honor,*
> *then honor.* Let no debt remain outstanding, *except the con-*
> *tinuing debt to love one another, for he who loves his fellowman*
> *has fulfilled the law.* (Rom. 13:7–8, emphasis mine)

The Bible makes clear debt is wrong, but what if you can't
get out of debt any quicker than you're already trying to?

I've hatched some pretty crazy schemes to get out of debt:
everything from buying bulk lotto tickets (yeah, but then I'd
have to part with some of my money in the first place) to
selling things I have around the house (forget it—it took me
too long to acquire them). That's why I laughed when I read
the story of Lothian Tom.

Tom was a young man who thought he was pretty clever.
He didn't like to work, so he devised some pretty successful
tactics to make a quick dollar. First, he stole his grandmother's black cow and convinced her to buy another. He
took her money to market, where he painted the stolen cow
white, then took it home to his grandmother as her investment. The gig went off without a hitch until his father noticed the white paint on the cow running off during a
rainstorm and gave Tom the beating of his life.

Next Tom went to town with a measurement for his
mother's coffin but told the coffin-maker sadly that he was

also told to collect a debt in town from a man who had recently disappeared. The coffin-maker gave him the money instead, and Tom had a grand old time at the local tavern until the next morning. The coffin-maker arrived at his parents' house with the coffin only to discover that Tom's mother—who answered the door in perfect health—was still alive. He then realized he was out the pretty penny he lent to Tom.

Finally Tom went to the shipyard to hire some harvesters. He promised a higher wage than any of them had made that year. After Tom bought them all breakfast, they eagerly signed on. He then explained:

> I do not know but there may be some of you honest men and some of you rogues; and as you are all to lie in one barn together, any of you who has got money, you will be surest to give it to me, and I'll mark it down in my book with your names, and what I receive from each of you, and you shall have it all again . . . when you receive your wages.[1]

Well, you can guess what happened. Tom collected a small fortune from the band of workers, dropped them off in someone *else's* field to work, and left, promising to buy them dinner.

He never went back.

Looks like Tom certainly knew how to turn a quick profit.

Ah—a quick profit. What I wouldn't give for one. My husband is swift to point out there is probably a hard lesson to be learned through all our struggles with money.

Yes, well, that's what I'm afraid of. That lesson is also a likely answer to the question, "Why isn't God getting rid of the debt quicker?"

But what *is* the lesson?

I tithe regularly. I keep hoping God will heap blessings on me for my faithfulness. Sometimes I feel like a kid marching up to the teacher's desk with a pompous grin, saying, "Here, I've finished my homework. I'd like an A, please."

Truthfully, I've come to expect a reward from God for tithing.

So what does God expect me to do with my money?

And short of hatching a scheme like Tom's to repay our obligations, how in the world will we ever get ahead?

Come to think of it, I know of this cow . . .

Love,

your in-debted daughter

❋

Dear dancing daughter:

Well, at least you were dancing *before* you started thinking about money! Now, you'll want to sit down because what I am about to say about money is no dancing matter.

You don't own anything. Let me repeat: you do not *own* a thing. God has placed you not in a position of ownership but of manager of the blessings He Himself bestows. And He expects us to take good care of those blessings because they are gifts to be used not *only* to take care of our needs, but also to advance the work of His kingdom.

Notice I said *needs*, not *wants*. Far too many of us get these confused. "I *want* the house in the country." Yes, but will a condo in town suffice? "I *want* that new SUV." Okay, but would a Ford Focus get you where you need to go? "I *want* my wardrobe to reflect this year's hem lengths." Does *anyone* ever really notice the current fashion trend, or will last year's dress do just as well?

Too many women juxtapose what they think they absolutely must have with what they absolutely *want*, and that, my dear, oftentimes creates the very debt you are talking about.

This idea of wanting bigger, better, and more is not new. Fairy tales are such terrific morality stories because they deal with the real struggles of life. The Brothers Grimm wrote a piece entitled "The Fairy's Two Gifts" that speaks directly to the struggle of materialism.

The story begins with a fairy disguised as a human dressed in ragged clothes. She made a visit to two different homes. The first home belonged to a rich man who had everything to make life more than comfortable. The fairy tested the man's heart by asking for a night's lodging. The rich man, noticing the outcast state of the visitor, refused the fairy entrance into his home, declaring he had far too many valuable things. "If I were to admit into my house everyone who knocks at my door, I should soon have to take the beggar's staff myself."[2]

Next she went to the home of a poor couple who not only took her in but also gave her their bed and fed her a big breakfast, contributing all they had. The fairy, when she noticed the faces of the poor people who "wore such a happy, contented expression that she was sorry to leave them," granted them three wishes.[3]

What would you wish for, daughter? More stuff? A Get Out of Debt Now card? And then, more stuff? The impoverished man in the fairy tale said something very important for a twenty-first-century girl living in a material world to hear: "What greater blessings can I wish for but that we two, as long as we live, may be healthy and strong, and that we may always have our simple daily wants provided for? I cannot think of a third wish."[4]

It was the fairy herself who then suggested a new and bigger home. The couple cried out that they "shall want for nothing more."[5] I don't think high credit-card debt would ever have been their problem. They had learned to be content with less. Herein lies one of the secrets of a happy life.

I cringe at the bumper sticker that says, "He who dies with the most toys wins." Nonsense. He who dies takes nothing with him. We enter this earthly experience in a naked, unencumbered state, and we leave it in the same condition. No one's real worth is predicated on what she owns or how much money she made. True wealth is found in the richness of a life lived out with a sense of divine purpose—of knowing God has given you the privilege of joining Him where He is already at work, and doing that work *for* and *with* Him. That's "being rich" in its truest definition.

Jesus knew the burden of earthly riches, which is why He gave us such a clear picture of the weight of wealth. Remember? It is easier, He said, for a water-holding mammal with one lump or two to move through a sewing implement than it is for a rich man to get to glory (Mark 10:25). In that same passage, the Bible says the man "went away sad, because he had great wealth" (v. 22). You see, money didn't make the man happy; rather it robbed him of the desire to have an abundant, eternal life.

In the Grimm brothers' story, the fairy also visited the house of a wealthy couple who, upon learning that the stranger was really a fairy who was in the business of granting wishes, begged her to grant them three wishes also. Despite their inhospitable nature, the fairy graciously agreed.

As the rich man rode along the road, dreaming about his three wishes and wanting so much more than he already had, he scolded his horse for prancing about. He grumbled that he wished its neck was broken. And what happened? You guessed it: boom! The horse dropped dead. Then the rich man had only two wishes.

He didn't want to lose his expensive riding equipment, so he continued on his way, dragging the heavy saddle and bridle. He started imagining his wife sitting in the cool comfort of his home, and he got angrier. He blurted out, "Ah! I wish this heavy saddle would slip from my back, and that she was sitting upon it, not able to move."[6]

No sooner had the words left his lips than the saddle disappeared from his back and was fixed permanently under his wife, who was sitting back at their comfortable home. The rich man found himself in the awful dilemma of deciding whether to wish for all the riches in the world to be his, or to wish that his wife be removed from the saddle. He wished, against his will, that his wife be set free, and the fairy instantly granted the wish. Net gain: zero. No new wealth, no new stuff, just a miserable experience based on greed that gained the man nothing but heartache.

God doesn't give us debt. We give it to ourselves. We are people who *want* more because we think more is better. We think more stuff will dull the pain of a boring life or an empty marriage, or that it will satisfy the coveting of our neighbor's goods. Experts on my radio show repeatedly tell me the average American has nineteen thousand dollars of credit-card debt, and depression is at an all-time high in this country. Do you think there just might be a connection between the two? I believe in many cases, yes.

Question: How do you eat an elephant? Answer: One bite at a time. Question: How do you get rid of debt? Answer: One dollar at a time.

Put the skids on anything but absolutely necessary spending. Get rid of the *want* for things. Learn to recognize the difference between *wants* and *needs*. Be faithful in your giving, not because you get something out of it, but because God told you to give. Trust Him. He told us He would provide: "My God will meet all your *needs* according to his glorious riches in Christ Jesus" (Phil. 4:19, emphasis mine).

Money is a tough subject, and it can wreak havoc in a marriage. Get it under control before it controls you. If you don't master money early on, it will certainly master you.

Now, pick up the Clorox and start singing, "He owns the cattle on a thousand hills!" Our God will provide what we need—and that *is* a reason for singing.

Love,

your mama

Mom:

Your reminder that God owns the cattle on a thousand hills was music to my ears (and a nice change from my steady diet of show tunes). I often need to be reminded that whatever problem I'm encountering, it's never beyond the scope of God's ability to solve it.

But I have to tell you, I disagree with some of your statements on debt.

You mentioned the distinction between wants and needs, and it's a pretty clear one, I think. But you also mentioned the failure to recognize that distinction is what gets people into debt in the first place.

Not always.

Let me explain.

I know nothing I have is really mine. There isn't a single possession that's going to find its way into heaven with me. But not all the debt I have is a result of my desire for the newest, the brightest, or the best, either. In fact, most of it isn't.

I'll give you an example by illustrating a path in my life that I traveled, and you didn't have to: I married with a mountain of student debt. You and Dad have both remarked that attending law school was one of the best decisions I've made. Does that also mean that signing those student loan forms was a good decision? We all prayed about the choices before me and felt God's leading was to graduate school. But we also knew the money wasn't there to pay for it outright, and loans were the inevitable result.

So, now what?

Here's another example: cars. I didn't want to buy *new* cars (and I use the term loosely here), believe me. I brought an old, paid-off Toyota into the marriage. Matt brought a beaten Ford Ranger truck with him. (Remember, we used to call it Big Blue? You could hear that thing coming a mile away!) We were content to drive those clunkers into the ground.

But a car accident forced us to purchase one, and a blown transmission forced us, eight short months later, to buy another. We bought two more used cars because they were an absolute necessity but we didn't want to shell out tons of money for a depreciating asset (a glorified hunk of steel, if you will). Yet we also didn't have the cash to buy those cars outright (not many people do when it comes to a purchase that big), and so—more loans.

So, now what?

I know there's a problem with materialism in our society (and trust me, I've got plenty to say on that later). I also know I don't make perfect monetary decisions. But there are lots of Christians out there who *do* try to make the absolute best decisions with their money. Some are so careful they border on stinginess!

You said God expects us to be good stewards of the blessings He's given us, and I know that. I know it means maintaining our cars, repairing our houses, making things last. I feel I know how to handle God's blessings. But what about the burdens? What about the inevitable challenges that come with living in a debt-crazed, you-can-finance-anything world?

What do the budgeters, the penny-savers, the used-car buyers, and the this-was-a-necessity-so-we-had-to-take-out-a-loan folk do with their money? What is the answer to the "Now what?" question?

You mentioned ending all but necessary spending, getting rid of the *want* for things, and being faithful in your giving. Okay, good first step. I'm going to propose a second step: let go. "And do not set your heart on what you will eat or drink; *do not worry about it. For the pagan world runs after all such things, and your Father knows that you need them.* But seek his kingdom, and these things will be given to you as well" (Luke 12:29–31, emphasis mine).

Take all the worry about debt, those perfect spending habits, that distinction between needs and wants, and that fantastic tithing record, and throw it away. *Nothing,* and I mean *nothing,* that we do with our money is going to change the way the Lord takes care of us.

Money and its consequences are an unfortunate but necessary part of this life. Sure, we may get ourselves into debt or make ridiculous purchases (like that fuchsia ball gown I absolutely *had* to have but have never worn—free will is a funny thing). We may also work our way up the corporate ladder into a life of wealth or win the Tither of the Year award. But thankfully, "The universe was formed at God's command" (Heb. 11:3), not ours. This means that whatever our plans, thoughts, aspirations, or fears about money, they don't matter a lick: "The Lord knows the thoughts of man; / he knows that they are futile" (Ps. 94:11).

Remember you used to tell me I ought to do all I could, and God would take care of the rest? Well, I was reminded of that today when I thought about debt. I asked you in my first letter how we could get ahead quicker. I guess that if you're doing all you can—that means tithing, paying your debts, being careful with your money, and not prioritizing material things the way the "pagans" do—then you really *can't* get ahead any quicker. This life isn't on our timetable, after all. It's on God's. And that probably means that debt of mine is here to stay for a while.

Or I could win the Publisher's Clearinghouse Sweepstakes tomorrow! Yippee!

Here's the part of letting go that I love: I can free-fall into God's promise to meet my needs, and because I've committed those needs to Him, I know He will always come through. There isn't a problem I have that He doesn't have a solution for.

Getting out of debt? That's *definitely* a "need."

I'm convinced He's going to meet that one, too.

Love,

Sarah

14

Gambling

Dearest one:

Have you ever bought a lotto ticket? You can be truthful with your old mom. Have you? If you have, you are probably not unlike millions of other Christian women who have done the same thing. The question, then, is not *have* you, but *should* you?

Whenever I do a program on gambling, the phones light up like a Christmas tree. Opinions on this subject seem to split right down the middle between those who think gambling is A-okay and those who oppose it.

I happen to fall in the latter category.

Since we are talking about money, let's talk about the abuse of our funds. Clearly excess debt is a poor use of money. Wanton materialism is also foolishness (more on this later). But I would add that gambling, in all its forms, is also wrong.

Think of the principle of gambling. You place a wager in the hopes of making more money, and you do it at high risk.

For example, if you bet on a horse race, you are betting the animal you choose will win, place, or show, thereby increasing your investment. If your horse doesn't come in first, second, or third, you tear up your ticket and count it a loss.

What about the slot machines or blackjack or even poker? As I travel around the country speaking, I have noticed a marked increase in the number of states that foster the growth of casinos. In some places, they cleverly call it "riverboat gambling." But think about what goes on in these places. The object is to get you to put money into a machine or bet it on a handful of cards in the hopes that it will be magically transformed into more money.

And don't forget, these establishments tend to be fast and loose with free alcoholic beverages. Ever wonder why? The endgame is to get your thinking so fuzzy you won't know when to stop placing more bets. Do you think these places exist to lose money? They exist, with ever-growing popularity, because more people lose than win. Yet so many of us are foolish enough to enter these places and willingly *give* them our money. The "gaming industry," as it likes to call itself, is a multibillion-dollar business built on the knowledge that you lose so much more than you win. So why do we do it?

Well, one reason might be that we all really do love fairy stories. We watch the evening news and hear of a couple struggling away at the daily grind. Suddenly, they are thrust into the limelight because *they* had the winning lotto ticket!

They are magically transformed from folks with an average income to multimillionaires by the sheer luck of some floating balls in a machine—from paupers to princes, from rags to riches, from the routine of work to the luxury of wealth.

Hey, if it can happen to them, why not us? So the next time we stop for gas or to pick up a gallon of milk on the way home from work, we grab a ticket or two. What harm could that do?

I interviewed a man once who described this as "mutual theft." Isn't that good? What he meant was that only one person can win, and the rest all lose. In theory, we enter into this arrangement with the full knowledge that almost all of the time we won't win. Yet we rationalize that if we did win, wouldn't it be worth it?

Aesop had an old story that illustrated the risk of losing substance by grasping at the shadow.

It happened that a Dog had got a piece of meat and was carrying it home in his mouth to eat it in peace. On the way home he had to cross a bridge across a running brook. As he crossed, he looked down and saw his own shadow reflected in the water beneath. Thinking it was another dog with another piece of meat, he made up his mind to have that also. So he made a snap at the shadow in the water, but as he opened his mouth the piece of meat fell out, dropped into the water and was never seen again.[1]

What a picture of gambling! The dog had his food for the day. But he wanted more, so grasping out of greed, he lost what he had and ended up with nothing. It's just like buying a lotto ticket or playing the slot machine or betting on the horses.

Money, working, and surviving are frequently tied together in Scripture. Paul said, "If a man will not work, he shall not eat" (2 Thess. 3:10). He was warning the early church about loafers. He was also trying to teach them to discern between those who thought they deserved a handout from those who truly needed a helping hand.

We are confused on the subject of work in this country. Because of the overwhelming desire for material wealth, we view our jobs as a necessary means to an end. But in so doing, we fail to see our jobs as the gift they are meant to be.

Work was part of God's plan for perfection. In Genesis 2:15 we are told God Himself was the first director of human resources: "The LORD God took the man and put him in the Garden of Eden to work it and take care of it." The first job was gardening, lest anyone think groundskeeping is a menial task! Work was and still should be seen as a gift.

Gambling is our way of avoiding work. We think, *If I make enough money, I won't have to work anymore*. Work provides us with a mission field, an opportunity to live among those who do not yet know the love of the Savior. It is also a way for us to "look well to the ways of our households" (see Prov. 31:27

NASB). So, our jobs, including our crabby bosses, the long hours, the salaries that are lower than we would like—yes, all of it is part of that gift.

So, my darling, do you gamble? Has the "What's the harm" justification crossed your mind while reading this? Are you crossing the bridge of life with some meat in your mouth, wanting more? Before you think of grabbing for the shadow, write me and let me know if you agree or disagree.

I love you—and you *can* bet on that!

Love,

Mom

Dear Mom:

Well, you wanted honesty, so here goes: yes, I've bought lotto tickets. I've also bet on horse races a few times and even played slot machines. My perspective on gambling is a little different from yours, it seems. I don't happen to view it as an abuse of our money—not in all contexts, anyway. I'll tell you why.

Let me start by saying that I *do* recognize some aspects of gambling can be problematic. I've been to a few casinos and watched senior citizens eagerly spend the totality of their Social Security checks on a single night of desperately hopeful

wagering. I also know that alcohol is comped at these establishments because the minute your judgment begins to blur,
you're more likely to drop another twenty bucks on the
table.

The whole act of gambling can also be addictive. I've
known people to *drive* hours to *sit* for hours in front of a
dealer who will smilingly take a thousand dollars over the
course of a night from a single patron (who *never* looks as
if he has that kind of money to spare, right?). Gambling is
one of those pastimes that appeals strongly to addictive
personalities. Why? Because it's hard to know when to
stop—particularly when you feel as if you're on a roll. You
can easily dismiss someone's recommendation to quit by
rationalizing, "Just a few more spins, and then I'm done."
At what point are you truly finished? How much do you
have to win (or lose) before you can turn it in for the
night?

Yet I view all forms of gambling as nothing more than entertainment. I must admit that it can be an expensive form of
entertainment. And perhaps a form that's not safe for everyone (remember what I said about those on fixed incomes, or
addictive personalities).

But I still see it as nothing more than a pastime. I don't see
the sin involved in placing some money on a horse race. In
fact, the excitement of an unknown outcome, the cheers of
the crowd, the thunder of horses' hooves can all combine to

make it worth every penny you've laid down on the hope of a happy result. Where's the harm in that?

I don't legitimately think I'm going to "hit it big," either. The best I've ever done was to win a few hundred dollars by hitting the trifecta on the Belmont Stakes last year. And while movies like *It Could Happen to You* (the one about the cop and the waitress who split their lottery winnings) make it look as if anything's possible, I'm not one to pin my hopes on a lotto ticket.

Why not? Well, because the odds are almost *always* against me (that's why they call it "betting," right? Otherwise, they'd call it "a sure thing"). You called it "mutual theft." Hmmm . . . is that why I've heard slot machines referred to as one-armed bandits? Proverbs 21:6 says: "A fortune made by a lying tongue / is a fleeting vapor and a deadly snare." But I think gambling is pretty up front, don't you? You know what you're getting, you know the odds, and you know what it's going to cost.

No lying there, right?

After all, it's exciting to think that something fortunate and unexpected could be right around the corner.

You mentioned the verse in 1 Thessalonians about working—a warning to loafers, right? Well, I don't rely on gambling as a substitute for, or even a supplement to, my income. I don't use it to avoid work; in fact, I think you know me to be a dedicated employee. I recognize the necessity of my job, but I also see it as a blessing from God: it feeds our family, pays our bills, and provides me with an opportunity to be a light in a dark environment. Plus, I work some pretty long hours. I don't think the loafer explanation is going to work with me.

And the Aesop fable about the dog? That dog was just plain dumb. Come on, we *all* know a steak in the hand is better than one in the water, right? That canine had a *sure thing!* It served him right to lose it. I think that dog was a *tad* greedier than I am, thank you very much. You're never going to catch me spending my paycheck on a night of gambling in the hopes of doubling my investment.

But a one-dollar lotto ticket? Well, that's another story.

I'm not an addictive personality, not on a fixed income, I spend almost nothing on gambling and hold a steady job that is my sole source of income.

Can you really tell me that in my case, it's all that bad?

Love,

your daughter, "Lucky"

Dear daughter:

I must be just as honest with you. I am not surprised. But I am disappointed. Since you are too old for me to ground you, I will persuade you with a sound argument instead.

You talk about the gambling you have done in the past and dress it in the argument of "What's the harm?" Here's where being a Christian calls you to a life of distinction. Maybe today, and for right now, gambling has not harmed you and your husband, but there are two other perspectives on this issue you have chosen to ignore.

First, you forget the beast you are feeding. The gaming industry comes into a state and lobbies lawmakers about the future revenues gained by gambling. It promises better highways and bigger schools, all gained by "easy money"—from you and anyone else who wants to pay for these improvements by means other than state taxes. Rarely, if ever, does the money go where it was promised, but by that point, it's too late. The gaming houses are entrenched, and once comfortably set, the giant is too big to move.

You, my darling, have now contributed to an industry that has ruined marriages, fed addictions, fostered felons, and funded crime. And you ask, "What's the harm?" You become a part of the problem, one dollar at a time—just like the vast number of others who also asked, "What's the harm?"

Second, there is the issue of your life as a living epistle. Other people watch you as a Christian, and they look for the hallmarks of distinction. What makes you different as a result of following that Savior from Nazareth? They might be observing your life choices, thinking, *She did it and didn't get hurt. I can do it, too, and not get hurt.*

But what if they *do* get hurt? What if they can't stop with just a few dollars here and there at the racetrack? What if the holiday on the cruise ship packed with casinos creates a habit they can't break? Do you think you have an obligation as an ambassador for Christ to your fellow man?

Do I sound too old-fashioned? Perhaps, but maybe this is where I get serious with you (and with me) about what it means to be *in* the world but not *of* it. Paul, in writing to the church at Galatia, wanted them to know what it meant to be free in Christ. He warned against satisfying "me" first: "You, my brothers, were called to be free. But do not use your freedom to indulge the sinful nature" (Gal. 5:13). Paul was pointing out that our liberty is not an excuse to feed the giant of selfishness in our lives.

This is a common struggle, fueled by the advertising world. Look at what Madison Avenue does to endorse that idea. "*You* deserve a break today" and "Frankly, *you're* worth it!" are popular slogans used to make us feel as if we exist for the sheer purpose of satisfying numero uno.

But the real liberty we have in Christ, Paul said in Galatians, comes from serving one another in love. "The entire law is summed up in a single command: 'Love your neighbor as yourself'" (5:14). Isn't it more loving to your neighbor to refrain from fostering an industry that has a history as well as a future potential of damaging lives, than it is to fund it?

You may have the liberty to go and pull the handle of the one-armed bandit, or you might have the luxury of taking a few of your hard-earned dollars and placing them on a thoroughbred at the racetrack. But what about the person who struggles in this area? You've helped to maintain a business built on hurting him. That is not loving your fellow man.

We are challenged as women of the Word to do what is good. Is it good to gamble? Not if it hurts one single person. Are we expected to earn a living rather than hope for a windfall? Without a doubt! And again, that work of ours is a gift! To do what is right, the Bible says, "is profitable." Going to a gambling establishment is not, nearly all of the time.

To me, gambling is very much like the story of "Little Red Riding Hood." This well-known tale is, in fact, a lesson of deception and a word portrait of things not always being what they seem.

The little village girl went to see her grandmother, who had given her a red cape. Once she was at her grandmother's house, she was "much astonished to find how different the old woman looked from ordinary."

"Grandmother, what great big arms you have!"

"That is to hug you better, my dear."

"Grandmother, what great big ears you have!"

"That is to hear you better, my dear."

"Grandmother, what great big eyes you have!"

"That is to see you better, my dear."

"Grandmother, what a great big mouth you have!"

"That is to eat you all up," cried the wicked wolf.[2]

Fortunately for the little village girl, a man rushed in and killed the wolf with his ax, and Little Red Riding Hood was saved.

Gambling is like the wolf. It disguises itself as something it is not.

"What great highways you will build," said the gambler. "The better to help your commute," said the gaming industry.

"What big schools you will build," said the blackjack player. "The better to help your child learn," said the casino.

"What great profits you will bring our state," said the lotto player. "The better to make someone a multimillionaire at the expense of millions of other poor fools," said the state lotto commission.

Darling, whose side are you on: the wolf's or Red Riding Hood's? Every penny you spend on gambling gives the wolf more of a reason to lunch on other poor souls. Stop feeding the wolf, and call for the man with the ax. It is not a harmless activity. Your liberty is hurting other people!

I am still your mother—and I still have a thing or two to teach you.

Love,

Mom

15

Materialism

Mama:

I'm sitting here listening to my husband sand the drywall in the living room. I'm impatient because we're still in the repair phase of this old farmhouse, and I want to move immediately into the nesting stage. I want to decorate and arrange, purchase and display, set up and set out.

Don't you just love nesting? There isn't a woman I've met who doesn't like to do it (whether or not she's even got a knack for it), because there's just something innately satisfying about feathering your nest. "Nests" and "feathers" are foreign concepts to men, you know. In fact, I can clock the seconds it takes Matt's face to fall when I chirp at him over coffee on a Saturday morning, "Okay, honey, only a few errands to run today: Bed, Bath & Beyond, Home Depot, JoAnn Fabrics, and the mall, if we've got time."

I might do better challenging him to a one-legged race through a minefield.

Or a leisurely swim through a crocodile-infested swamp, perhaps.

Why is the desire to nest so inherently female? Why do we women invest in our houses with time, effort, and money—lots of money? Money we make at work that goes right back into our houses, for curtains and knickknacks and furniture. Oh, and sometimes our cars. And yes, occasionally the crisp Ann Taylor suit we just knew would be perfect for next week's office party, the vanilla-bean lotion that smelled so sweet at Bath & Body Works, the silver candlesticks from Macy's that we knew would look smashing in the dining room . . .

Excuse me, I digress.

I've heard it said that clichés are clichés because they're true. Maybe there's something to this "women and shopping" thing after all.

I work to help pay off debt and contribute to the support of our family. But running a close second for motivation is working to buy: cars, clothes, and yes, things for the house. Does that make me materialistic?

I mean, would anyone work for the sake of working if she absolutely *didn't* have to?

My friends carry Kate Spade handbags, wear Donna Karan clothes, and sleep in Pottery Barn beds on Berber carpet. Are we all big, clueless sinners for wanting (or more important, having) nice things?

Do you remember the goose that laid the golden eggs in the film *Willy Wonka and the Chocolate Factory?* I'm reminded of that phrase "golden goose," but rarely does anyone realize that the original story of that priceless bird didn't start with a goose at all:

> There was once a man who had three sons, and the youngest, who was called Simpleton, was constantly mocked, disdained, and slighted. Now, one day it happened that the oldest brother decided to go into the forest to chop wood, and before he went, his mother gave him a nice, fine pancake and a bottle of wine so that he would not have to suffer from hunger or thirst. When he reached the forest, he met a gray old dwarf, who wished him good day and said, "Give me a piece of the pancake from your pocket, and let me have a drink of wine. I'm very hungry and thirsty." However, the clever son answered, "If I give you my pancake and my wine, then I won't have anything for myself. So get out of my way," and he left the old dwarf standing there.[1]

Understandably, the dwarf didn't take too kindly to the fact that he'd been rudely rebuffed, and with a little magic, he saw to it that when the clever son was chopping wood, he solidly whacked his arm with the ax, forcing him to return home. Shortly thereafter, the second son appeared, and the same scene transpired, with the son claiming that "whatever I give you, I'll be taking from myself. So get out of my way."[2]

Again, the increasingly cantankerous dwarf made sure the son cut his leg while chopping wood, and the injured young man quickly returned to his family.

Soon enough, Simpleton made his own way into the forest and encountered the same gray dwarf, who asked if he might partake of Simpleton's food and drink because he was so hungry and thirsty. Now, Simpleton (clearly *not* the favored son) had been given only a pancake made out of water and ashes and a bottle of sour beer—not terribly enticing. But as one might expect, it was the "simple" one of the bunch who acted just as he ought to and shared everything he had, though it wasn't much, with the dwarf. The dwarf was warmed by his kindness and responded, "Since you have such a good heart and gladly share what you have, I'm going to grant you some good luck."[3]

That luck turned out to be the discovery of a goose with feathers of pure gold that made him instantly wealthier than he ever dreamed possible.

Why is it that those who have so much are often so unwilling to part with it? The older brothers had fresh pancakes and expensive wine yet wouldn't dream of parting with even a morsel. Their youngest brother, the simpleton with the sour beer and ash pancake, was unthinkingly generous.

Of course, *I* like to think that if I were prosperous, I'd be quick to donate, give, and distribute.

Yes . . . me and the rest of the innumerable masses hoping for unexpected wealth.

When the rich young ruler in Matthew 19:16–22 asked Jesus what he had to do to inherit eternal life, it could be said that he was fairly materialistic. Not just because he "had great wealth" (v. 22), but because when Jesus told him to "sell your possessions and give to the poor, and you will have treasure in heaven. Then come, follow me" (v. 21), the young man's disappointment was obvious and immediate—and he sadly turned down Jesus' offer on the spot.

I'd previously made up my mind that materialism isn't about *having* great wealth but being unwilling to part with it: in other words, making your possessions and prosperity the most important aspect of your life. But now I'm not so sure. Could it be that having wealth in itself is the real problem?

Mom, help me figure out where my desire for nice things crosses the line.

And hurry up—I've got one foot out the door to the mall!

Love,

your daughter

Daughter of my heart:

Don't laugh when I mention this, but remember the TV special *Mr. Magoo's Christmas*? It was a modern cartoon rendition of Charles Dickens's *A Christmas Carol*.

Mr. Magoo, as Ebenezer Scrooge, sang "Jingle, jangle, coins when they jingle make such a lovely sound." The song encapsulates the love of money. You remember in this classic Christmas story that Scrooge, prior to his transformation and redemption after encountering three ghosts, had a problem with money. He loved it more than anything else. He loved it to the exclusion of family and friends. He counted it daily and nightly. He underpaid his assistant, Bob Cratchit, and offered no gifts to charities when they came calling. He had lots of money, and he was miserable.

Paul talked about the struggle we all have with materialism in his letter to Timothy. This letter is still amazingly apropos, particularly for us twenty-first-century Christian women. He challenged us to remember that we "brought nothing into the world, and we can take nothing out of it" (1 Tim. 6:7). If "stuff" were so important, wouldn't God have made a way for us to pack it all up and take it with us when we die? If our worth and value were predicated on the acquisition of things, then surely the great King would have created a kind of divine yardstick that measured our worthiness on the volume of what we have acquired. He didn't, so that is our first hint that "stuff" is not all it's cracked up to be. But contentment is another matter.

Paul told us that being content is "great gain" (1 Tim.

6:6). Listen to how he defined contentment: "But if we have food and clothing, we will be content with that" (v. 8). No Donna Karan clothes mentioned anywhere in that passage. The staples of a diet Timothy and Paul would have had were bread, olive oil, fish, and sometimes a bit of beef, pork, or fowl. Pretty basic. Clothing would have been plain and simple.

In his second letter to Timothy, Paul requested that his coat be brought because winter was coming (2 Tim. 4:13). His coat—not *coats*. No fashion statements, no symbols of status, but a garment to keep him from shivering in prison.

This traveling missionary had learned to be content with so little. That convicts me more than you could possibly know. Madonna was right when she sang, "We are living in a material world," and I struggle not to join her on the rest of the chorus, "and I am a material girl."

Paul reminded Timothy and us that "people who want to get rich fall into temptation and a trap and into many foolish and harmful desires that plunge men into ruin and destruction" (1 Tim. 6:9). Our basic nature is to want more, and yet, as we conform to the image of Christ, it is amazing how we can learn to be content with less.

Let me go back to your golden goose idea. Old Aesop, with his minimorality tale, "The Goose That Laid the Golden Eggs," articulated the greed that resides in the human heart.

One day a countryman going to the nest of his Goose found there an egg all yellow and glittering. When he took it up it was as heavy as lead and he was going to throw it away, because he thought a trick had been played on him. But he took it home on second thought, and soon found to his delight that it was an egg made of pure gold. Every morning the same thing occurred, and he soon became rich by selling his eggs. As he grew rich he grew greedy; and thinking to get at once all the gold the Goose could give, he killed it and opened it only to find nothing there.[4]

The countryman is a picture of someone who so lusts after more that he abandons contentment in the process. Paul said that some people are so eager for money they walk away from God and "pierce themselves with many griefs" (1 Tim. 6:10). Notice Paul wasn't saying that God brings about the heartache, but rather we bring that heartache upon ourselves.

I heard a psychologist on a TV program say that women, more than men, use shopping as a way of dealing with depression—a kind of temporary euphoria that momentarily takes away the darkness in our souls. But it is a deal made with the devil, because the same doctor said after the high of shopping, we go into a deeper depression. We recognize the stuff not only didn't fill the hole in the heart, it made the hole bigger.

It is the *love* of money that really is the root of all kinds of evil. Making money or material goods your god causes you to turn away from your first love. Greed and the desire for more have ruined marriages, corporations, and political leaders. You and I are not above this temptation. So how do we flee the ensnaring net of materialism?

Having wealth, in and of itself, is not a problem. Having nice things is not a sin, either.

Making money and material goods your reason for living is. Here's a measurement to use to guard your heart in this area. Ask yourself some questions:

1. Do you love you stuff more than God? A good test is where you spend more time—in the Word or in the mall? Are you hungry after the stuff in your catalogs, or the stuff of God's principles and precepts?
2. Where do you spend your money? Your check register is a great litmus test for where your priorities lie. Are you supporting more ministries than you are your favorite merchants? Do you give beyond that 10 percent, which is supposed to be a starting point, not a definitive figure?
3. What stuff would you be willing to give up? You can't take it with you anyway, so why does it take such priority now in your life?

I think of the story of the Chinese Christian sister who is currently in a labor camp because of her faith in Jesus. She is required to make seven hundred hand-knotted ornaments a day. That's *seven hundred*—no exceptions. Some days she is up at 4:30 in the morning and works until late into the night, only to repeat the same menial task the next day. Yet reports have come out of that prison saying that she sings while she knots the thread. Sings! She has nothing—nothing except Jesus—and *she is content.*

Just as you must balance your checkbook, guard your heart by keeping the *need* to help provide income for your family and the *want* for nice things secondary to the desire to keep the Lord the most important thing in your life. He and He alone can give you real contentment. Because of His unconditional love, our "account" in heaven can never be "overdrawn."

So, speaking of materialism, how do you keep that old love of money from taking root in the garden of your heart?

Love,

your mama

Mom:

After reading your letter, I have better tools for determining when my desire for nice things crosses the line.

But that "love of money" thing? Well, that's going to be a harder question to answer than it looks at first glance.

I know a few things about my spending habits now. For example, I know I *don't* love my things more than God. I love them, to be sure (I really *hate* it when I break a dish, tear a hem, or lose a trinket), but I try to remind myself constantly that they'll be worm food, fertilizer, or the foundation for a high-rise condo development in another hundred years or so.

I also know if I'm truthful, I split my money equally between God and the outlet malls (I used to think that was really something—I mean, I spend *a lot* at the malls!). And while I'm consistent in tithing, it *is* a struggle sometimes to give more than 10 percent. I know if I had to, I would give everything up (but I can't promise I would do it without complaining; I haven't *quite* mastered Philippians 2:14 yet).

So, if I think I'm doing generally pretty well in handling our cash flow, how do I know when the love of money has actually taken root in my life? That's kind of like trying to determine at what point someone got cancer—like all evil things, it often starts out completely unnoticed, quiet, insidious.

The love-of-money's sneaky entrance may have been why the Lord repeatedly warned against it. It could be why He made a point of remarking on it repeatedly, as if to say, "Keep your eye out for this one, because it can spring up before you know it."

Think about this: aside from the warnings in 1 Timothy, there's the lesson in Matthew 6:24: "No one can serve two masters. Either he will hate the one and love the other, or he will be devoted to the one and despise the other. You cannot serve both God and money." And how about James 5:1–3? That's a pretty severe warning for those tempted by wealth: "Now listen, you rich people, weep and wail because of the misery that is coming upon you" (v.1).

"Hate." "Weep[ing] and wail[ing]." "Misery." Who'd have thought that something as useful, basic, and necessary as money would have the potential to be so bad?

This makes me think there may be a way to determine when the love of money has slipped through the front door of my life and made itself comfortable on the sofa. When that happens, things start to get sticky.

Let me take you back to *my* golden goose fable and pick up where we left off, with old Simpleton in the woods. You remember he was given a golden goose for his generosity to the dwarf. Well, after the encounter, he made his way to an inn where he intended to spend the night:

Now, the innkeeper had three daughters, and when they saw the goose, they were curious to know what kind of strange bird it was. Moreover, they each wanted to have one of its golden feathers. The oldest thought, I'll surely find an opportunity to pluck one of its feathers. At one point Simpleton went out, and she seized the goose by its wing, but her hand and fingers remained stuck to it. Soon afterward the second sister came and also intended to pluck a golden feather. However, no sooner did she touch her sister than she became stuck to her. Finally, the third sister came with the same intention, but the other two screamed, "Keep away!" . . . But . . . she ran over, and when she touched her sister, she became stuck to her, and all three had to spend the night with the goose.[5]

Here's what I've learned about greed: it seems pretty harmless at first. In fact, it might just look like simple desire: *Oh, wouldn't it be nice if I had* . . . But the bigger that desire grows, the more powerful it becomes, and at a certain point I think it's impossible to squelch. It has a tendency to sweep everything—and everyone—into its wake.

Each of those sisters was motivated by her own desire for a gold feather. None heeded the warnings of the others until finally all three ended up permanently stuck to the goose and each other. The greed of one made the greed of the next one that much harder to stifle.

So, how do I know when the weed of greed has taken over the garden of my heart? When money becomes more important than memories. When I'm counting dollars instead of blessings. When I'm playing the "He who dies with the most toys wins" game. In other words, when I get truly "stuck" on the idea of buying, getting, and spending.

Simpleton, the hero of our story, was the only one who managed to maintain a proper perspective on the goose. He didn't try to pluck its feathers, cut it open (hoping to find golden eggs), or sell it for a profit. No, he simply realized it was a temporary gift, an unexpected blessing that made his life more enjoyable for as long as he had it—and nothing more.

Money is a necessary evil of our lives on this earth. I think the key to mastering it is to take the lead from the name of our fairy tale hero: Simpleton. Not that we should be stupid about money, but we should be innocent, and "simple" about what is *really* important.

> Do not store up for yourselves treasures on earth, where moth and rust destroy, and where thieves break in and steal. But store up for yourselves treasures in heaven, where moth and rust do not destroy, and where thieves do not break in and steal. For where your treasure is, there your heart will be also. (MATT. 6:19–21)

After all, even golden geese eventually die.

But a life lived for Christ—that we *can* take with us.

Love,

your daughter

"Deeper meaning resides in the fairy tales told to me in my childhood than in any truth that is taught in life."

—JOHANN C. FRIEDRICH VON SCHILLER

The Final Fairy Tale

Deeper meanings transform fairy tales from childhood stories into lessons for living. And even though we may be all grown up, we still find ourselves experiencing what so many of our favorite storybook characters experienced: running from the wolf of a devouring culture; praying to break the spell of sin brought to a garden by a dark and evil prince; being brave and courageous when faced with the giants of disappointment and disillusionment; and finally, waiting for the One true Prince who will take us away.

As grown women, we don't have to abandon fairy tales. Rather, we can rediscover we are living in the midst of the greatest story of all. We can choose to let life so overwhelm us that we lose our way in the dark and scary wood of earthly living, or we can raise our faces to the Son and let Him illuminate our paths until we arrive safely home.

For us, the fairy dust never really settles. We *are* able to fly because we've been told that those who "hope in the LORD / . . . will soar on wings like eagles" (Isa. 40:31). Peter Pan said, "All you need is trust and a little bit of pixie dust." In fact, all we need is trust and the reminder that we *are* real-life princesses, the daughters of the most high and glorious King who will someday take us to live with Him in a magnificent mansion, located in the city on a hill.

Perhaps this book has challenged you to rediscover some of the great lessons from the fairy tales of the past. But if I may, let me ask you to read just *one* more: a modern tale, but a fairy tale, nonetheless. In it, may you find the fairy dust that will wing you on your way to the knowledge that life *is* the great fairy tale—and that we have the blessing not of not reading it but of *living* it.

The Final Fairy Tale

Once upon a time . . .

. . . there lived a little girl with flaxen hair named Anna in a kingdom called Detroit. Anna was a princess, though to her chagrin, the rest of the world (including the resident king and queen) simply hadn't caught on to that yet. Anna didn't mind. She was secure in the knowledge that her tree house was her castle and her dolls her subjects. Her beagle, Jake, was her noble steed (though she discovered the hard way that Jake didn't make the best mount).

Anna had what might be called a preoccupation with fairy tales. It wasn't enough to simply watch Disney's *Little Mermaid* a few times, or to build an impenetrable fortress from a refrigerator shipping box. Oh, no. Anna fell asleep every night to the tune of "Someday My Prince Will Come" squeaking inharmoniously from the music box on her nightstand. She named the sections of her mother's garden as provinces in Annaland. And she requested that her family and friends refer to her as "Your Ladyship" and occasionally "Your Highness" (though the latter required a particularly obnoxious mood).

Anna was the heroine of her own great story, and her family and friends, though thinking it somewhat odd, tolerated and even indulged it for the sake of the pretty girl's happiness. For the princess, life was good.

And then a funny thing happened.

The princess grew up and the battlements of her kingdom's walls started to crumble.

It began in high school. In the middle of her sophomore year the king and queen filed for divorce. Suddenly she had not one family, but two, and the warring factions never ceased their battling. Holidays represented compromise, not celebration. Birthdays became chances for the king and queen to outshine one another. Anna's performances in recitals and track meets were opportunities for her parents to prove their parenting skills, not applaud the achievements of their daughter. Despite Anna's best efforts to think otherwise, the king and queen had become two very ugly trolls.

Then, in college, the prince she thought had come to rescue her turned out to be a lecherous deadbeat (no matter how many times she heard it, she still believed "I forgot my wallet"). He instilled in Anna a sense of shame that plagued her the rest of her life.

Of course, there were the mounting student loans, too (the "dragons," she called them); the loss of her first job (the "black plague"); the eviction from her second apartment (the "club-wielding giant"); and the car accident that left her with a shattered collarbone and pins in her leg (because of its "magic," she called this one the "evil wizard." How else could an eighteen-wheeler manage a 180 degree hairpin turn in the middle of a crowded intersection and land *precisely* on her car?).

Despite life's hard realities, Anna clung fast to the notion that everything was going to work out in her favor—that there was, somehow, a guiding force in her life that would lead her to fulfillment of the dreams that came traipsing happily after her into adulthood.

So she waited.

And she waited.

And then, she got married.

It was a beautiful but small ceremony. Small, because the king and queen had fought so feverishly about the division of their contributions for the wedding that the princess and her prince (a fellow named Mark), in the end, paid for it entirely themselves. For the period of a few brief months, Anna thought the tide had turned, and that her fairy tale had in fact come true.

But her elation didn't last for long. There was the unexpected pregnancy (twins, nonetheless), the loss of the prince's mother to cancer, and his job transfer that resulted in the small family's relocation to the foreign and distant sovereignty of Cedar Rapids.

Because day care was expensive and there weren't many eligible employers for her profession in Iowa, the princess gave up her job as a public relations executive to stay home full-time with the boys. She spent her days at home alone, save for two vexatious twenty-six-month-olds, dirty laundry, and a whole lot of *Sesame Street*. Each day, Anna's life lost its luster a little more.

But you can't take the fairy tale out of the princess. You see, the myth doesn't die, not for those who really believe it. All you can do is try to convince her that she isn't really a princess after all.

For Anna, that was precisely what happened.

One rainy day in the heartland, Anna woke up to the babies crying, the dog whimpering, and the smoke alarm beeping its angry reminder that the dryer vent had gotten clogged again. She peeled her weary eyes open, stumbled into the bathroom, and stared into the mirror.

Some princess, she thought. *A scullery maid is more like it.*

That day began like any other, with breakfast, errands, and the laundry during naptime, but sometime between the dishes and dinner preparations, Anna noticed a snow-white dove perched on the branch of an elm outside. *Funny*, she thought. She had never seen a white dove in the wild—only in a magic show or at the zoo.

Anna turned from the kitchen window without another thought until a strange sound brought her back—the bird's call. It wasn't a call, really, but something else, something beyond the rhythmic "oooh–ooooh"-ing one would expect from a dove. This bird's "song" wasn't musical in the least. In fact it sounded like . . . *words*. It was almost as if the creature was trying to communicate something.

Oh, please, Anna chided herself. *Has my life really become so bland that now I'm hearing birds talk? I've simply watched one* Barney *episode too many, that's all.*

But the next day, by the same sink, after the same dishes, and before the same dinner preparations, Anna looked up from the pot she was drying and saw the same white bird perched on the lowest bough of her elm.

She looked at her watch. It read 4:42 PM. The same time she had seen the bird the day before. The hair stood up on her arms as she watched the creature with the funny voice turn its head quizzically from side to side, its beak opening and closing with rhythmic precision. Was he actually trying to speak?

Anna told Mark about the bird that night, about the odd occurrence of his presence at 4:42, about his voice that sounded eerily human. Without looking up from his *USA Today*, Mark mumbled, "Mmmm, sounds nice, dear."

"And I cooked the dog to make a casserole for the neighbors," she added cheerfully.

"Good, honey. That sounds nice."

It figures that he doesn't want to listen to me, Anna thought. *What about my life could possibly be more engaging than what he's reading? Nothing.*

At 4:42 the next day, Anna stopped her vacuuming and went to the sink, hoping beyond hope that the little white bird had found some other homemaker to annoy.

She was disappointed to learn he hadn't.

Her patience tested, Anna threw open the window and leaned out. "Shoo!" she hissed. "Get out of here, you little vermin!"

And then something remarkable happened.

The white bird turned to her, opened his beak, and with perfect clarity said "The King!"

Anna pulled her head back in the window so quickly she caught it on the sash, eliciting a howl and temporarily silencing her squawking twins in the other room. She closed her eyes and rubbed her head, thinking, *I just imagined that. I've got to get myself under control.*

When she opened her eyes, the bird was no longer sitting on the elm branch, but on the window ledge directly in front of Anna. She was so startled she stumbled backwards, tripped over the dog, and landed squarely in his water dish with an utterly graceless thud.

The bird opened his orange beak again: "The King is coming."

It was like a promise, a question, and an answer all in one.

Anna lay on the floor, stunned. She was hallucinating, right?

"The King is coming."

There—he said it again. If this was the bad pizza she had eaten for lunch, it had an awfully loud voice.

Despite her better judgment, Anna mustered the courage to say something back. "Uh . . . what king?"

Silence.

"What king?"

But in a flurry of snowy wings, the bird departed, leaving Anna on the floor, in the dog's water dish, with a throbbing headache and the sense that something terribly important was going to happen.

At 4:29 PM the next day, Anna was at the window. She waited.

She swept the floor.

She waited.

She scrubbed the sink.

She waited.

Finally, at 4:42 the white messenger made his appearance again. Anna threw the window open with gusto. "What king? Who? Why are you coming here to tell me this?"

Bird looked at her silently, bobbing his head up and down and side to side. He looked so common, so unremarkable, that Anna started to wonder if the whole talking-bird occurrence had been a delusion she manufactured to deal with the utter mundaneness of her life.

She had begun to retreat from the window when the bird opened his beak:

> I know of a King, the one you seek.
> He desires the lowly, the contrite, the meek.
> He sees your life, and his heart is pleased,
> On life's next journey, your burdens he'll ease.
> A princess you are, in the land of a King,
> This life of toil is the perfect thing,
> To practice the skills he instilled in you,
> And bind your hearts till this life is through.

Then, as quickly as he had appeared, the snow-white bird departed without so much as a feather to mark his passing.

Anna stood dumbfounded at the window *A princess*. The word echoed in her head like a firework. Anna, the scullery

maid from Cedar Rapids, was royalty after all. She felt as if
someone had just turned on the lights in the dark house of
her life.

In a moment, Anna was running to the study and picking
up the Bible that had gotten dusty from neglect those many
years she'd spent in servitude. Despite the fact that she had
forgotten where to look, she somehow managed to stumble
upon the book of Jeremiah:

> Who should not revere you,
>   O King of the nations?
> This is your due.
>   Among all the wise men of the nations
>   and in all their kingdoms,
> there is no one like you. (10:7)

How much she had forgotten since she was a child. How
far away those promises of her inheritance as the daughter of
a King had seemed to her, as life's trolls and giants, dragons
and evil wizards had sought to steal her joy, right along with
the awareness of who she truly was.

But no longer.

Anna couldn't wait to share the news with Mark that day.
When he returned from work, and the dinner was eaten and
the boys fast asleep, Anna and Mark talked late into the night.
They talked about the bird's promise and what they themselves had forgotten in the maze of their own life choices and

hardships. They talked about their dreams, their sacrifices, and their destiny as children of the King.

As the night waned, Mark turned to his wife, her blonde ponytail sagging, dishrag in hand, and reminded her, "I love you, Anna."

Anna smiled coyly back at him. "Don't you mean, 'Your Highness'?"

And so it was that the prince and princess lived happily ever after. Until, that is, they went home to the King.

It was then that the highest and greatest happiness of all the world began.

The End

Notes

Chapter 1

1. Armand Eisen, ed., *A Treasury of Children's Literature* (Boston: Houghton Mifflin Co., 1992), 262.

Chapter 3

1. http://abc.go.com/primetime/extrememakeover/show.html (26 February 2004).
2. http://abc.go.com/primetime/extrememakeover/bios/dana.html (8 October 2003).
3. http://abc.go.com/primetime/extrememakeover/show.html (8 October 2003).
4. Amy Wallace, "Jamie Lee Curtis: True Thighs," *More*, September 2002, as quoted at http://www.lhj.com/lhj/story.jhtml?storyid=/templatedata/lhj/story/data/jamieleecurtistruethighs_08212002.xml (29 February 2004).
5. William Goldman, *The Princess Bride* (New York: Ballantine Books, 1973), 34.
6. Ibid., 56.

Notes

235

Chapter 4

1. Leslie Bennetts, "Deconstructing Jennifer, *Vanity Fair*, May 2001, as quoted at http://www.angelfire.com/tv2/Friendsobssession/article-vanityfair.html (29 February 2004).
2. Alice Mills, ed., *The Random House Children's Treasury* (New York: Random House, 2003), 241.
3. Blaise Pascal, *Pensees and Other Writings* (New York: Oxford University Press, 1992), 36.

Chapter 5

1. The Brothers Grimm, *Grimms' Fairy Tales* (Ann Arbor, Mich.: State Street Press, undated), 234.
2. Ibid., 235.

Chapter 6

1. Jack Zipes, ed., *Complete Fairy Tales of the Brothers Grimm* (New York: Bantam Books, 1987), 706.
2. Ibid., 706.
3. Ibid., 642–43.
4. Albert M. Wells, Jr., ed., *Inspiring Quotations* (Nashville: Thomas Nelson, 1988), 59.
5. Zipes, *Complete Fairy Tales*, 642.

Chapter 7

1. Eisen, *Treasury of Children's Literature*, 290.
2. Ibid., 292.
3. Wells, *Inspiring Quotations*, 123.
4. Ibid., 93.

5. George Sweeting, ed., *Great Quotes and Illustrations*, (Waco, TX: Word Books, 1985), 179.

6. As quoted in Gilbert Meilaender, "Men and Women–Can We Be Friends?" *First Things* 34 (June/July 1993): 13-14.

Chapter 8

1. Eisen, *Treasury of Children's Literature*, 112.

2. Zipes, *Complete Fairy Tales*, 143.

3. Ibid., 144.

4. Eisen, *Treasury of Children's Literature*, 20.

Chapter 9

1. Mills, *Random House Children's Treasury*, 173.

Chapter 10

1. http://cdc.gov/od/spotlight/nwhw/allstages.htm (29 February 2004).

2. http://ohiolife.org/abortion/index.asp (29 February 2004).

3. Mills, *Random House Children's Treasury*, 399.

4. R. Nisbet Bain, ed., *Russian Fairy Tales* (New York: Funk & Wagnall's Company, 1927), 17.

5. Ibid., 18-20.

6. Mills, *Random House Children's Treasury*, 400.

Chapter 11

1. Zipes, *Complete Fairy Tales*, 2.

2. Ibid., 2–3.

3. Ibid., 4.
4. Ibid., 4.

Chapter 12

1. http://www.heritage.org (29 February 2004).
2. http://www.allianceformarriage.org (29 February 2004).
3. Mills, *Random House Children's Treasury*, 194–195.
4. Ibid.
5. http://www.afa.net/pornography/GetArticle.asp?id=99 (11 December 2003).
6. Thomas Bulfinch, *The Age of Fable* (New York: Review of Reviews, 1913) as quoted at http://www.bartleby.com/bulfinch/ (February 28, 2004).
7. Mills, *Random House Children's Treasury*, 359.
8. Ibid.

Chapter 13

1. *Scottish Fairy Tales* (London: Senate, 1995), 405.
2. Mills, *Random House Children's Treasury*, 353.
3. Ibid., 353.
4. Ibid., 354.
5. Ibid., 354.
6. Ibid., 355.

Chapter 14

1. Mills, *Random House Children's Treasury*, 394.
2. Ibid., 303.

Chapter 15

1. Zipes, *Complete Fairy Tales*, 256.
2. Ibid., 257.
3. Ibid.
4. Mills, *Random House Children's Treasury*, 395.
5. Zipes, *Complete Fairy Tales*, 257–258.

About the Authors

JANET PARSHALL is the host of *Janet Parshall's America*, a Salem Radio Network nationally syndicated program originating from Washington, D.C. *Janet Parshall's America* is one of the few conservative talk shows in America hosted by a woman. Janet has also been profiled as one of the top 100 talkers in *Talkers Magazine*, the leading trade publication of the talk industry, every year since 1998. In addition to *Janet Parshall's America*, Janet hosted *Renewing the Heart*, a radio program dedicated to women's issues produced by Focus on the Family from 2000 to 2003.

As a radio and television commentator, author, and advocate for the family, Janet is much sought after nationwide to speak on public policy issues that impact family preservation and promotion. She has appeared on numerous national television and radio programs, including *Crossfire, Hardball, Nightline, The Larry King Show, Donahue, The 700 Club, Late Night with Aaron Brown*, and various other shows on CBS, NBC, ABC, CNN, MSNBC, CNBC, CBN, PBS, the BBC, and NPR. Janet has also been featured in *People* magazine.

Janet and her husband, Craig, have coauthored three books, *Tough Faith: Trusting God in Troubled Times, The Light in the City: Why Christians Must Advance and Not Retreat,* and *Traveling a Pilgrim's Path: Preparing Your Child to Navigate the Journey of Faith.* The Parshalls live in Virginia and have four grown children and a growing number of grandchildren.

SARAH PARSHALL PERRY received her B.S. in Journalism and a double minor in French and Vocal Performance from Liberty University in 1995, where she acted as feature articles editor for the *Liberty Champion*. She then received her J.D. from the University of Virginia in 1999, where she was on the editorial board of the *Virginia Journal of International Law*. After graduation, Sarah went on to practice as a civil litigation attorney with a small firm in Baltimore, Maryland, before joining the advertising and marketing ranks as in-house counsel and marketing manager for a Baltimore advertising agency. Sarah has had various works published by the International Society of Poets and has been actively involved in youth ministry for the past ten years. Sarah and her husband, Matt, live in Baltimore County.